CRITICAL & *Creative* THINKING

STRATEGIES FOR CLASSROOM INQUIRY

SUSAN WILKS

D1616826

Heinemann
Portsmouth, NH

First published in 1995

Heinemann
A division of Reed Elsevier Inc.
361 Hanover Street
Portsmouth, NH 03801-3912

Offices and agents throughout the world

Copyright © 1995 Susan Wilks

All rights reserved. No part of this publication, except those pages indicated, may be reproduced or transmitted in any form or by any means, electronic or mechanical, including photocopying, recording or any other information storage and retrieval system, without the prior permission in writing from the publisher.

ISBN 0 435 08869 6

Published simultaneously in the United States
in 1995 by Heinemann
and in Australia by
Eleanor Curtain Publishing
906 Malvern Road
Armadale, Australia 3143

Production by Sylvana Scannapiego, Island Graphics
Edited by Ruth Siems
Designed by David Constable
Cover photograph by Sara Curtain
Printed in Australia by Impact Printing

The evidence thus far suggests that students who have been exposed to philosophy are more reasonable and more thoughtful, and that their teachers are not merely better at teaching specific subjects, but also are more effective in developing general thinking skills. These are two significant contributions that teaching philosophy can make to education. A third is the potential of philosophy to modify our conception of education. Rather than conceiving of education as helping children acquire the knowledge that adults possess, we might begin to recognize that a central objective of education is to create communities of inquiry, through which children learn to value independent and autonomous thinking. (Lipman 1985)

Contents

Acknowledgements

My thinking on the connection between the possibility of improving approaches to thinking and inquiry in schools has been influenced by many writers and colleagues. Matthew Lipman, whose influence remains a dominant force in the field, first conceived the idea of using philosophical issues and approaches with children in the 1960s and wrote a series of texts for classrooms over two decades. For five years I trialled his 'Philosophy For Children' program in many schools. Discoveries of new and complementary approaches as I worked with teachers and their students led to this book.

Other colleagues: Andrea Baster, Brenda Cherednichenko, Cheryl Iser, May Leckey, Susan Schudmak and Sandy Yule, have provided ongoing support. Teachers who offered their classrooms for extended periods—Fred Carstens, Di Greenway, Adam Kenny and Chris Pearce at Yarra Valley Anglican School, and Helen Williams and staff at Deepdene Primary School—have played a major role in the formulation of classroom approaches represented in this book. The timely meeting with Tom Jackson in 1990, and endless ideological arguments with Laurance Splitter helped me clarify my beliefs about using philosophy in schools. I also wish to thank the many other practitioners, too many to name, with whom I have conversed and reflected.

The support of my family, especially Bob, Peter, and Lewis, has been constant and vital.

Preface

Thinking occurs in a social context and is influenced by culture and environment. In order to build on their experiences successfully, students need to have well-developed thinking skills. If we wish our students to become effective participants in society we need to assist them to develop a range of skills which give them practice in reflective and critical thinking.

Personal development involves becoming aware of, and valuing, our thoughts and feelings and those of others. Teachers can assist this process through a philosophical inquiry approach and by providing activities which foster the analysis and clarification of values and appropriate social action.

In 1988, my work in educational philosophy with fourth-year Bachelor of Education students was proving a difficult task. They were resisting participation in discussions about social issues which I felt were relevant to trainee teachers about to start work in schools. Questions such as 'What will you do if your values clash with those of the school community?' were met with retorts like 'We'll leave that sort of discussion to the humanities staff.'

On probing, it became evident the students felt that there must be a right answer, which they did not know. If someone disagreed with an individual's point of view, it was often taken as a personal affront. Many were reluctant to participate in discussions about ethical issues which they saw as having no obvious answer; they would not express a personal opinion in front of peers for fear of disagreement or disapproval, and were not good at listening to others' opinions if they differed from their own. I was dismayed that this was the case after they had undergone sixteen years of formal education.

At this time I heard about a program in philosophy for children developed by Professor Matthew Lipman, a philosopher in an American state college, which was based around a philosophical 'community of inquiry' approach. With dialogue at the centre of its methodology, the program looked as though it had the potential to develop the skills the BEd students needed in order to engage in discussions which were considered both appropriate and necessary. Its stated aims were:

- to stimulate students to think well
- to improve students' cognitive skills so they could reason well together
- to challenge students to think about important ethical and social concepts
- to develop their ability to think for themselves so they might think autonomously about moral problems

The work of the philosophers Peirce and Dewey provided important theoretical foundations for Lipman's program. Central in Peirce's writing was the concept of a 'community of inquirers'. By this he meant that, no matter what your country of origin, if you are a physicist, a chemist, or a mathematician then you belong to a larger-than-national community of thought.

In Dewey's writing, Lipman found a pedagogy for converting classrooms into such communities of inquiry. He was also influenced by Dewey's insistence on the importance of experience in learning — both the experience the students bring to a classroom, and the stimulating and relevant experience which is to be provided in the classroom. During the 1970s and 80s Lipman wrote stories for school-aged students which contained philosophical issues appropriate for student discussion. Issues such as truth, fairness and equality were raised in the texts.

My work in schools has been primarily to test to what extent school-aged students are capable of sophisticated abstract thought. I also needed to observe whether the skills of thinking and dialogue that Lipman believed are developed in a community of inquiry did, in fact, develop. It was necessary to find appropriate resources for teachers and their students to use during these sessions, and to establish the extent to which teachers could cope with, or recognise when they were doing, philosophy with their classes.

It was also important to ascertain whether, by using the community of inquiry method, philosophy would fit into and across the existing curriculum and improve other disciplines. Was it feasible to expect students to question both their surroundings and their progress in discussions?

It was found that the use of the community of inquiry developed the skills of dialogue and thinking listed above. I now encourage the teachers with whom I work to teach their curriculum disciplines in a reflective and philosophic manner using this method of procedure. This involves the teachers and their students becoming cooperative and caring co-inquirers.

Today, many Australian teachers are working with the skills of philosophy in a systematic way. Most begin by using materials which have been specially designed to introduce philosophical issues and skills. As their confidence grows, teachers include other resources which they believe will raise appropriate issues. The community of inquiry model, which promotes excellent skills of thinking and dialogue, remains the central feature of classes.

This book is an account of teaching strategies found to be successful when establishing a community of inquiry at a variety of levels. It also describes changes in teachers' roles and in students' responses. Perhaps the best comments come from the students themselves.

Adriana Guiffrida, a year 6 Melbourne student, when asked to describe her involvement in philosophical inquiry said:

> You can share your feelings about a subject and can disagree with someone without hurting their feelings. This approach prepares you for when you are older because it gives you the courage to speak up. It's different from other subjects because it's fun. Sometimes there is a big debate and you hear interesting and funny opinions. Sometimes people mix up what they are trying to say and it comes out all wrong. It also teaches you to listen and that is a good quality to have.

Susan Wilks

CHAPTER ONE

The Role of Inquiry

When educators in Australia and other countries talk about using philosophy in the classroom they may variously mean using the skills of philosophy, examining ethical issues, working with specially written resource materials, or any 'traditional' philosophy being taken in schools.

The use of philosophical inquiry as a means of developing the skills of dialogue and thinking involves teachers and their students in becoming cooperative and caring co-inquirers working together in a community of inquiry.

Moving on from Bloom and Piaget

Piaget's stage theory attempted to explain the thinking of young children. Although most useful in its provision of ways of understanding how thinking abilities develop through stages, it was too limiting because it suggested that because children think concretely in their early years, their instruction during this period should likewise be concrete rather than encouraging abstract thinking.

When Bloom formulated his taxonomy of educational objectives in the 1950s, he described thinking skills as developing sequentially, implying that higher order thinking, like analysing, reasoning and evaluating, were beyond younger students. The consequence of the theories of Bloom and Piaget is that younger children have not normally been encouraged to think abstractly or to reason.

There are, however, implications of Piaget's stage theory that should be noted:

- To the extent that language facilitates and guides thought processes, students should be given ample opportunity to interact verbally, not only with teachers, but with one another.
- To the extent that concepts arise from exploring the environment,

students should be involved in real and relevant activities.

- Insofar as development proceeds from understanding the concrete to the symbolic, curriculum activities should move from manipulation of the concrete to the symbolic.
- To the extent that teachers understand the progression of logical thoughts, they can provide activities appropriate to developmental levels and also provide appropriate challenges.

Work being done every day in classes using the community of inquiry to engage in discussions of philosophical issues demonstrates that children can deal with abstractions long before the onset of Piaget's so-called 'formal stage'. With a growing emphasis on the importance of inquiry learning, cooperative group work and development of the individual, the education process has enabled philosophy to become meaningful.

Children begin to think philosophically when they begin to ask 'why?' It is this process that is encouraged and nurtured in the community of inquiry. Its approach provides students with the intellectual tools they need. It provides a model of procedure that is appropriate for the various disciplines a student is exposed to during the course of the school day. When a community of inquiry has been established, teachers become the

The teacher becomes the facilitator rather than the sole source of information.

facilitator rather than the source of information to whom the students look for affirmation.

Thinking skills must be taught

Sometimes we assume that students can reason, inquire and form concepts without having been taught the necessary thinking skills.

But the teaching of such skills, often through consideration of ethical issues, must occur with aims and desired outcomes clearly present in the mind of the teacher. Whether it is called 'community of inquiry', 'philosophy', 'English/language' or simply 'thinking', it is the rigor of its application, the intention on the part of the teacher to see that it does happen that is of prime importance.

Although subject disciplines today include problems of everyday life, we need to focus specifically on how we might go about improving our students' skills of thinking and dialogue. This can begin in specially defined sessions, but gradually a more general transfer across the curriculum will occur.

SOME FALLACIES ABOUT TEACHING THINKING

According to Edward de Bono, the creator of the term 'lateral' thinking, the following four fallacies are associated with the claim that educators must be teaching thinking skills if they are teaching thinking.

1 Intelligence is the same as having thinking skills.
This is not the case. Intelligence is potential, not necessarily good thinking. Highly intelligent students may be good at problem solving and reactive thinking, but less able in the kind of thinking that requires them to seek out and assess e.g. figuring out why a car has broken down.

2 Teaching knowledge is sufficient.
Definitely not so. Knowledge is only gained and applied when it is meaningful. Good thinking skills are essential to make the best use of knowledge.

3 Thinking skills are taught in every subject.
Partly true. However, the skills that are learned are, in the main, limited to information sorting, analysis and debating skills. Teachers are less likely to be promoting the thinking skills involved in decision making — prioritising, seeking alternatives and considering other people's views

4 Any thinking will develop better thinking.
Merely practising a skill, such as two finger typing, only reinforces existing habits. The improvement of thinking must be systematically approached.

Improving thinking and dialogue skills

A community of inquiry emerges from frequent group discussions fostered by teachers who are committed to the process of inquiry. The students set the agenda for discussion, and the skills are not given to them by the teacher but drawn from them via discussion. This means that we, as teachers, need to know what we are looking for.

If we want better thinking to occur in the classroom we should expect reasons to be given when statements are made. Our thinking, and that of our students, should be self-correcting. We should review what we say and look for mistakes in our reasoning:

> *'No, wait a minute, I'm wrong there ...'*

We should help students to isolate and practise good thinking skills:

> *'See how Lee followed on from Sam's point ...'*
> *'Are you being consistent there?'*

Being precise when searching for good reasons adds rigor to discussions, for example:

> *'Are you agreeing with Simone?'*

or

> *'Isn't that a contradiction?'*

Reading and writing can be seen as natural outgrowths of conversation, which is the child's natural mode of communication. A well-structured community of inquiry should emphasise:

- linking reading, conversation and writing
- the use of resources (literature, film, music) which includes experiences that are meaningful to the students
- wondering about the complexities and puzzles of everyday life
- the examination of words that are critical to our use of language, such as 'seems' and 'like'

Students are capable of recognising the circumstances that call for appropriate use of skills, such as when it is best to ask a question and when it is important to point out an assumption. This ability is only acquired by practice, and classroom dialogue is the mode of obtaining such practice. We therefore need to ensure that classroom discussions are providing practice in the thinking skills we are aiming to develop.

The nature of the community of inquiry ensures that children develop an awareness of the process of inquiry by being encouraged to ask questions like:

'Are you saying you think …?'

and to restate points with statements like

'I think Adam is saying … but I disagree.'

Through an exposure to a variety of points of view, children come to recognise there are many interpretations of any piece of information.

The need to clarify meanings is a vital prerequisite for good communication. The extent to which this occurs in the classroom depends on how much we encourage such a process. The community of inquiry reveals the importance of clarifying one's own terms by accurate communication.

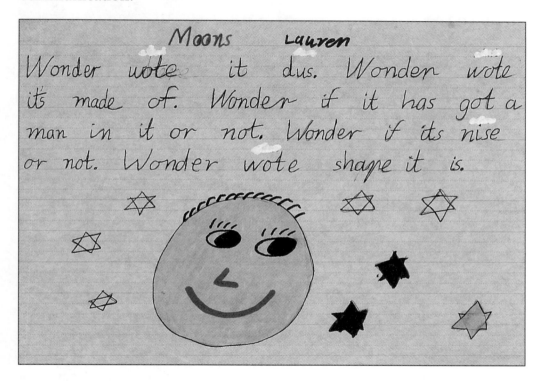

Lauren's questions about the moon

The nature of philosophical conversation

In a community of inquiry, whatever the stimulus for a discussion, whether it is reading a text or viewing a video, the source material should be shared. It provides the group with a common starting point. The public activity of talking and reading is linked with the private activity of thinking via dialogue. Reading to oneself in class is not the same.

Ronald Reed, an educational philosopher long associated with philosophical inquiry in schools, wrote that a conversation should be

Ronald Reed discussing fairness and equality with year 6 students

'earnest yet playful, and demonstrate a free-flowing curiosity' (Reed 1992). He stressed that it is important to focus on specific problems or issues whilst recognising they may not necessarily progress in a neat or linear fashion. Conversations thrive on being of a non-linear, amorphous quality. They thrive on repetition, reflection and redundancy, and involve the handing around of ideas from person to person.

Conversations allow for the incorporation of two models of teacher–student relationships, one in which the teacher has the necessary knowledge and dispenses it to the students, and the model of a community of inquiry where teachers and students share the solution of problems.

A flexible conversation puts the focus on the interest and sense of involvement of its participants and so helps them stay 'on task'. Following their interests determines the direction the conversation takes. People are free to accept or reject the invitation to join a conversation. At best one can invite and encourage participation.

Transfer of skills across the curriculum

Discussion skills learned in the community of inquiry setting transfer readily across the curriculum. For example:

- improved reasoning is connected with improved reading for meaning

- the ability to make assumptions and inferences from texts, normally via discussions, enhances the meaning of what is read in any subject
- philosophical inquiry deals with a wide range of issues and attempts to correct and improve thinking about these issues via discussions that are not exclusive or specific to any one discipline
- participants learn that different problems require different responses and that some can be resolved, some temporarily resolved and others have no resolution

Because of the methodology of the community of inquiry, there is no need to create a new space in the curriculum, or exclude another subject when introducing philosophical inquiry into the curriculum. Because of its language content and subject matter, the program fits most comfortably into the primary school language/social issues areas of the curriculum and the secondary school English curriculum. The areas of social justice, humanities, mathematics and science are enhanced when the community of inquiry method is applied.

Developing independent thinkers

Any parental or societal objections to the idea of classes working with the issues of philosophy hinge on the notion that by developing independent thinking the program may encourage students to reject the values of home and society. Implicit in the objections are the following assumptions:

- Children think that home or society's views are no good.
- Children will reject existing values when they discuss them, whether they believe them or not.
- Children will adopt 'wrong' standards and become amoral.

However, rather than indoctrination occurring, precisely the opposite is the case. It is only when students are given sets of values and not equipped to assess them that indoctrination occurs. The community of inquiry approach ensures that all experiences and points of view are respected.

When philosophical reasoning is brought to bear on a problem, the probability of critical appraisal and the formulation of constructive ideas is increased. The discourse promotes an environment which is sensitive to philosophical issues and others' points of view. This is a crucial setting for the formation of unbiased attitudes and the appreciation that others' opinions can also be substantiated by sound reasoning.

It is the very capacity to think independently and reflectively that will ensure that values are held with the required commitment, and if learning is to be successful, it must be capable of withstanding critical assessment. Teachers do not foster philosophy to undermine beliefs, nor erode values, but to help children build foundations and frameworks for their existing beliefs.

Philosophy's contribution is that it grapples with a wealth of ideas and demonstrates that there are many interpretations of any issue, and such knowledge should enable children to reason about any view that is forced on them. Involving parents in sessions similar to those their children are experiencing is the best way to answer or prevent criticism.

Teachers as facilitators of inquiry

Can we expect a conversation to build its own dynamics? It may not build at all. Merely monitoring a dialogue is not philosophical inquiry. It is easy to fall into the trap of trying to clarify every word or concept, but the other extreme is to not take on the responsibility of fostering the discussion.

The teacher's role is to facilitate the inquiry, which works best when all members of the group participate. Each member of a community of inquiry needs the opportunity to translate the experience into something meaningful for them. Having one's ideas examined is a personally rewarding experience, even when agreement is not achieved.

Classroom analysis of philosophical inquiry

Some recent analysis of classroom dialogue has highlighted the benefits of philosophical inquiry. Christine Perrott, a teacher educator at the University of New England, looked at learning quality by examining classroom talk in a regular primary classroom session and a philosophy session and analysed both the content and form of the discourse. (Perrott 1988)

In her introduction she notes that much of the talk in classrooms 'is not conducive to the development of inquiring, orally competent and thoughtful persons'. She went on to say that she believed that the community of inquiry approach could be a useful way of breaking out of the binds of classroom talk as it is now widely carried out, in that it places the emphasis on developing ways of thinking in students rather than on transmitting subject matter to them.

Perrott believed the emphasis on classrooms as inquiry contexts, rather than places of instruction of curriculum content, was important. She was interested in observing a community of inquiry to find out about:

- the relationships between participants
- the way knowledge and learning were presented and produced

- the rules the participants accepted as appropriate to that context
- the contents exchanged in the discourse
- student language and thinking

She noted the benefits:

> The teacher explicitly asks pupils to become information givers ... It appears that there is a shift in relationships, roles and agendas. ... it is not a matter of listening to and commenting upon knowledge from the 'expert', or even of trying to answer a question put by the 'expert'. Rather it is a case of knowledge and questions from the 'inexpert', the curious ones, the ones who don't know or who dare to disagree, and are prepared to express this publicly. ... such behavior in regular class sessions is relatively rare ...
>
> ... as well as a shift in agenda ... there is evidence that because the content has been turned over to the pupils there is an increase in interest and thus genuine curiosity.
>
> ... personal interest appears to have been aroused by the experience of talking and listening to a partner in a hub-bub situation. A pupil not only considers an interesting angle to this listening and talking but is, it seems, encouraged to intervene publicly with this consideration.

These observations highlight a prime achievement of the conversations of the community of inquiry method: the provision of a suitable environment for ideas and questions to be aired. Perrott also noted that the transcripts from these sessions 'illustrate pupils moving towards an inquiry mode and teachers away from a transmission instructor mode'.

ADVANTAGES OF THE INQUIRY MODE

Perrott lists the advantages of the inquiry mode over the transmission instructor mode, claiming that the former results in:

- relatively large amount of pupil talk
- extended pupil answers
- breaking out of the teacher–pupil–teacher pattern of talk
- lack of teacher manipulation towards a certain response or content coverage
- shift in role of teacher from that of expert information giver to that of listener
- non-curriculum content topics pursued
- teacher questions which have no 'right' answer
- the emergence of pertinent and thoughtful pupil questioning

Other teachers have noted similar features emerging in their students' discussions. Susan, a year 3 teacher, wrote that she believed her students' thought processes had developed. She mentioned that she had regular discussions in class and that, whereas in the past they would argue with undeveloped ideas, they had now begun to reason, and were prepared to 'diverge'. The sessions had been particularly valuable for one class member who was not academically strong, yet had blossomed during the sessions, as had many other students. The 'emergence' of students previously not challenged to contribute is often noted by teachers as one of the most rewarding aspects of the inquiry.

John, a year 6 teacher who had used philosophical inquiry for three of his twenty-five years of teaching, identified three main areas of change. Firstly, he said, he had not explored issues to the same extent in the past, particularly ethical concepts. Secondly, he had not previously dreamed of doing conceptual analysis at this level. And thirdly, not only were his students displaying higher order thinking skills, they were always able to *recognise* the improvement in their discussion and listening skills.

> ## Thought and Thinking
>
> Thought to me is more of a past tense than thinking. Like you are more likely to say I had a thought and thinking is something you do at the present time
>
> You still could use them the other way round but most people would perhaps write it in the above way.
>
> Thought also could perhaps be deeper than thinking and thinking might be something you just do in maths or when you are asked a question but thought you consentra deeper on.

CHAPTER TWO

Encouraging Pupil Participation

The community of inquiry provides a supportive and nurturing environment which fosters reasoning and critical and creative thinking. Classes gather (usually in a circle) to discuss a variety of philosophical issues where teacher and students are co-inquirers; the teacher is the facilitator of discussions, while the students identify the issues for discussion. The process is as important as the subject matter and develops cognitive skills such as:

- the tolerance of others' opinions
- the ability to recognise and assess value judgements
- the development of problem-solving strategies
- being able to see what is relevant in a given context
- self-critical thinking
- the ability to recognise sound and faulty reasoning
- the habit of defining terms and justifying statements

Some introductory activities

The activities and exercises outlined below encourage participation in creative and critical thinking. They act as tools to aid students' verbal inquiry within a supportive setting and introduce distinctions that are helpful in making sense of basic philosophic questions during the establishment of the community of inquiry.

WHAT IS A GOOD DISCUSSION?

This exercise helps a class to focus on the important aspects of a discussion. (Suitable for years 3–6).

1 What is the purpose of a discussion? Are there rules for good discussions?
2 Is it ever okay to criticise the person who says something, rather than what they said?

3 Should we always be expected to give reasons for our opinions? Can you think of a time when it wouldn't be expected?

4 Can you think of a time when you could ignore another person's opinion if it was not the same as your own?

5 Should we offer to drop our opinion if it is not the same as everyone else's?

It is important to think carefully about each of the points. Elements of a good discussion might include: one person speaking at a time, hands up to indicate you want to speak, asking for clarification if necessary, etc. The second point deals with an essential skill: the ability to confine one's reaction to a statement to what has been said, rather than the person who said it. With number three, there may be times when a person should not be required to give a reason for an opinion, for example if it meant they would have to divulge family secrets. When considering point four, students could be encouraged to give examples of a time when it might be all right to ignore another's opinion.

One would hope that there would come a time when any student would hold on to their opinion, even if they were a lone voice. Point number five provides the opportunity for this to be discussed, and could lead to the identification of occasions when students would be prepared to change their opinion, for example when more evidence is presented, further reading is done, or when someone is able to successfully convince them of the strengths of a counter view.

■ DISCUSSIONS AND OPINIONS

One year 6 teacher designed a '*Discussions and Opinions*' handout talking about good discussions with his class. It featured Snoopy saying: 'I think that dogs should be allowed to drive cars, go to the movies and eat at McDonald's' and Lucy replying, 'That's the dumbest thing I ever heard, you bonehead. Anyway, who cares what you think?'

The teacher posed these questions for consideration:

- What is the purpose of a discussion?
- What are the rules for good discussions?
- How would Snoopy feel after Lucy's comments to him?
- What should happen to those who go against the rules for discussions?

Some of the rules of discussion suggested by the class were:

- No-one should yell or call out.
- You need to concentrate on what others are saying.

- You should say what you think or feel.
- There should be no put-downs.
- You should be able to state your opinion freely.
- Let others finish what they want to say.
- Raise your hand if you want to speak.

■ HOW SHOULD WE TALK TOGETHER?

Teachers of students in kindergarten to year 2 could use this simplified version.

1. Put up our hand first.
2. Speak in turn.
3. Crawl around the classroom floor.
4. Yell at each other.
5. Say what we find interesting in a story.
6. Not bother to wait for people to finish speaking.
7. Not give a reason for what we say.
8. Laugh if someone forgets what they were going to say.

■ RULES

This activity demonstrates how 'rules', a topic which is relevant to students, was handled by a year 2 class. The extract is from Paul Jennings' book *The Cabbage Patch Fib*.

> Dad hadn't noticed because he was too busy pretending not to be watching *Doctor Who* on the TV. It is a rule in our family that the TV is not on at tea time, but somehow or other Dad never notices it is on until *Doctor Who* is over.

The students asked the following questions about the extract, which were then written on the blackboard. The class chose to begin their discussion by examining the second question.

1 What is a rule?
2 Is there a reason for all rules?
3 Are all the rules in families made up by the parents or can children invent rules?
4 When is it all right to break a rule?
5 Are they some rules which should be broken?
6 What happens to rules when nobody obeys them?
7 Is it really a rule if the teacher/ Dad/ your friend never obeys it?

Children constantly have rules imposed on them, but rarely think about the purpose of a rule, or even what constitutes a rule. When using the community of inquiry model, reflective thinking is a primary goal. The thinker is required to consider an issue through discussions with classmates and teacher, often formulating alternative circumstances and considering the meaning that same issue would then have. Although thinking is generally an internal dialogue, the 'community' provides a suitable means for advancing thinking.

A vital benefit of this method is the self-esteem of individuals. They become aware that their opinions are listened to and respected. Members of the group are willing to wait for the slower contributors to formulate their ideas, and will help if requested.

THINKING ABOUT THINKING

Experience in many classrooms has shown the benefits of spending a few weeks immersed in a variety of creative and rigorous activities. Activities like those below ensure that the class is working with abstract concepts and being challenged to find creative solutions.

■ THINKING

1 Can you remember something that happened to you at pre-school? Are you remembering or imagining this event? How can you tell?

2 What are you thinking about right now? Could anyone know what you are thinking just by looking at you?

Name
NICK

Thought and Thinking

The words thought and thinking have a similar meaning, but I believe that the word thought has a stronger meaning. Thinking can be just thinking about anything to do with the subject in your mind at that minute. Thought is when you focus on a problem that has arisen or something more definite than just thinking about a number of things that are in your mind. Thoughts are more powerful than just thinking, it sort of is trying to get deeper in to your mind. So thoughts and thinking are nearly the same but I believe that thoughts are a stronger thing.

3 Where are your thoughts stored? Are they in color?

4 Think of your front door at home. How can one person make another person think about a particular thing? Could someone make you think a sad thought? Is it the same kind of thought as a thought of a door?

Any one of these questions may result in a discussion which lasts for quite some time if contributions and disagreements from class members are invited. The activity encourages students to be reflective about the thinking process. They become accustomed to discussing abstract concepts and are therefore prepared for later sessions using literature.

STUDENT PERCEPTIONS

A group of year 6 students who had been involved in a few sessions of introductory exercises were asked to answer three questions about early skill developing sessions they had been involved:

1   What is the point?

2   What was the interest level?

3   Any further comments?

Student 1

Q1   *What is the point?*

A   I thought the point of it all was to try to use our minds and to try to think about difficult questions.

Q2   *Interest level?*

A   I thought that the activities were very interesting. I liked the big questions ... interesting because we tried to think of a solution to the problem.

Q3   *Any other comments?*

A   I thought it was very useful to the grade because we had never done this kind of work before.

Student 2

Q1   *What is the point?*

A   I think that the point was to try and get us to stretch our minds and our way of thinking. I think it will help us in life because we will be able to look at issues from different points of view.

Q2   *Interest level?*

A   I think that the interest level is made higher by using more mature material that we can relate to.

Q3   *Any other comments?*

A   I think that the way that we went about it, e.g. large discussions and then personal work, was the best way to approach it.

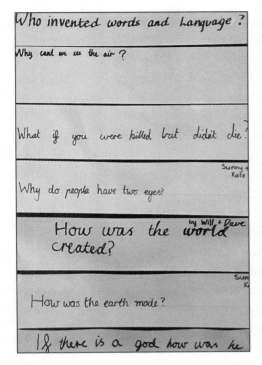

The students' questions become the focus for inquiry

Encouraging students to participate

It is important that we find ways of encouraging all students to contribute, think well, and have respect for others' opinions and thinking styles. 'Fast' thinkers tend to dominate discussions in both classrooms and other arenas of public discussion, but while some people can talk as they think, others need to toss ideas around in their head before they speak and this latter group is often excluded from discussion. They are too slow, the discussion moves on, and their chance to contribute is lost. They adapt to being the listeners.

The fast talkers may enjoy thrashing out points of logic or other topics of little interest to the majority of the group. Because they are quick to contribute, it is often their topics of interest that are discussed, and other members of the group are excluded once again. If students are turned off by the topic they will not contribute to the discussion.

By employing strategies that are inclusive of all members of the group we can combat these difficulties. It is important to include the fast talkers, but as equal participants, not dominators.

STRATEGIES FOR INCLUSION

A variety of grouping strategies help to combat domination and reluctance. Such groups may comprise:

- a mixture of good contributors and non-contributors
- a group of people who do not normally contribute
- a group of fast thinkers

Setting part of the class to work on associated written tasks is another strategy. This means discussion group sizes can be varied and varieties of participants selected.

An effective method used to discourage dominant talkers is to distribute five matches (buttons, marbles) to each member of the class prior to a discussion. Have them place one match into the centre of the discussion circle (or towards the front of their desk, depending on the classroom arrangements) each time they speak. Surprise! Some people use their matches quickly, others use none.

Another method is to create an inner circle of discussion participants one day, with an outer circle of observers. The observers can be directed to watch for many things, depending on the particular groups' strengths and weaknesses. For instance, students could count the number of times individuals speak, or time their contributions. Discussion of the findings will depend on what the teacher is trying to achieve.

Encouraging students to chat with those nearby about a specific question is an effective way of getting ideas to flow with everyone involved. Specific invitations to speak like:

Ideas flow when students chat about specific questions

Would you like to add something Anne?'

or

'What do you think about what Judy said, Tony?'

is another way of encouraging participation.

QUESTIONS TO ENCOURAGE PARTICIPATION

The following questions are posed in the style known as 'Socratic questioning'. (Paul 1993; Lipman, Sharp & Oscouyan 1980) This is because they probe the underlying structure of our thinking.

Learning to use questions like those below during a discussion encourages student participation. They focus on the process of the discussion, and when employed by teachers, shift the emphasis away from the teacher and on to the students.

- Does anyone else find that unusual?
- Can someone help Eliana to rephrase that question?
- Is that what you meant?
- Could you provide more information so we can answer that?
- What reasons can you give for saying that?
- Are Sam and Lee saying the same thing?
- Are those two statements of yours consistent?
- Have we made any progress?
- Who's still confused?
- Can someone summarise the discussion so far?

These questions focus on practical and specific ways of posing and responding to questions raised during discussion. They also help the teacher move on if they feel that they are hearing too many anecdotes or they are stuck on one issue.

Some activities, like the one below, are so stimulating that good group discussions are guaranteed. Students will remain on task, because it is a challenging exercise which requires definitions, clarifications and explanations.

ACTIVITIES FOR ENCOURAGING RELUCTANT PARTICIPANTS

Teachers often ask questions like:

- What do we do if the students don't attempt to answer questions or do not become involved in discussions?
- Should we ask shy students and those who are slow to respond?
- How do we help students to develop the skill of asking questions?

The following activities encourage reluctant participants in classroom discussions to express an opinion. Answers can't be judged by others as right or wrong, because a personal preference is asked for.

■ 1 A MEMORABLE EVENT

Describe an event like the school fair which would involve memory, experience, and interpretation. Have the class consider the following three features surrounding the event. In this instance:

1. The fair itself — the crowd, stalls, rides, etc.
2. Photographs they had taken
3. Their memory of the event.

Ask students which feature they believe would be the most valuable aspect for them. They should be able to provide reasons for their opinion. Encourage them to agree or disagree with other people's points of view. Check whether anyone changed their opinion after having heard another's reasons for a particular preference. (Based on Lipman 1974, p.45)

■ 2 ASKING QUESTIONS

When students are reluctant to contribute to a discussion you might be able to facilitate their involvement by giving them the responsibility of asking a question during a discussion. For example:

What makes you say that?
How do you know?
What is your reason for saying that?

Older students could ask:

What are we to conclude from what you are saying?
What are you assuming?

This activity also encourages students to track the discussion by listening to what is being said, because they are looking for an opportunity to ask their question at an appropriate time.

■ 3 WORDS THAT DESCRIBE THINKING

Ask students to brainstorm words which describe different ways of thinking. Write them on the board. (Perhaps sketch a head and write the words around it.) Students may at first not think of many words, but given time, words like *remember, calculate, imagine, infer* and *wonder* will surface. Try asking a question like: 'Which do you prefer, imagining or remembering?' and discover the kind of discussion that results. You could follow with a further question: 'Is it possible to imagine without relying on your memory?'

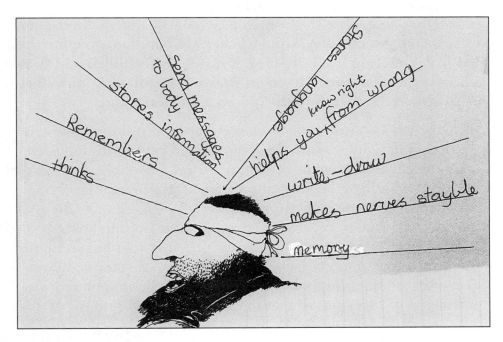

Students list words that describe thinking

◼ 4 POSSIBILITIES

Most students try to redefine all the statements so that they can be a reality. The necessity to define terms like *language, run* and *plays* in order to deal with the statements gives some idea of the strength of the exercise. Which of the following statements describe a possibility. Could they also be realities?

1. A dream comes true.
2. Steam engines run on ice-cream.
3. A person speaks the same language as everyone else.
4. A video machine plays films that have not yet been made.
5. Your friend is both older than you and younger than you.

Students enjoy discussing this type of question. The benefits of such an activity are that:

- challenging questions are being asked
- listening skills are being developed
- thinking skills are being developed
- dialogue skills are being developed

LEARNING TO WAIT

A technique that has been employed to involve reluctant participants is merely to wait for an answer much longer than is 'normal'. In a supportive community of inquiry environment, where students have come to know that what they say will be valued, this relatively simple strategy is most successful. A skilful teacher will build on any effort at all, so that if the offering is a little thin, it can be embellished and incorporated into the discussion. It doesn't take long for that individual to participate more frequently as the following demonstrates.

> Jason was not contributing in class either by answering questions or opting into discussions. The teacher had previously discussed with the class the benefits of waiting for responses because she wanted and valued a contribution from all class members. The teacher asked Jason a question. After a l – o – n – g wait (the teacher and class were very patient), he came up with an excellent example as part of the discussion. After that he put up his hand and contributed in a positive way on two further occasions. The classroom teacher said she previously had not bothered waiting and she expected that the student would opt out.

Another method which encourages participation is to give more reserved children a piece of card with a question/statement written on it, for example:
Encourage them to try to use such questions during the discussion. Of

How do you know that?	What are you assuming?	What is your reason for saying that?

course there is usually nothing wrong with simply asking Sam and Kim what they think about a certain topic. Just remember to wait a little longer for the answer!

Dealing with prior expectations

Teachers and students can carry preconceived ideas of what is expected from each other and of how a classroom should operate. When expectations of student performance are unprejudiced, the more reluctant contributor feels more confident about responding to the challenge to contribute. Following one discussion session a teacher who had been observing me take her class said: 'I nearly died when you asked Bobbie an incredibly complex question, and she answered it. I would never have asked her such a question.'

When there are no prior expectations of capabilities or contributions the invitation to participate is more open. Teachers have made the following comments:

- Annie now has something to say on each subject because she knows we will listen.
- Billie enthusiastically wants to be involved because her opinion is valued.
- Con's creative comments no longer are seen as clowning, but a springboard for further discussion, thus greatly increasing his self-esteem and others' regard for him.

The following report was written by a teacher working with the inquiry method for the first time. It describes the students' attitudes to new classroom procedures which accompany the community of inquiry approach of closely examining texts for issues. She noted that the students were 'constitutionally unable to sit with the idea' of spending an extended amount of time looking at the various issues that arise. She commented:

> I feel that this attitude is inevitable in schools as we know them — the kids have been so inducted into the mode of getting something done and moving on to the next thing as opposed to thoughtfully mulling over, going round questions, looking for implications.
>
> The instrumental approach is at the heart of our schooling — so we can't blame the kids for having accepted it. They are praised for the speed with which they can perform, not for the depth of the reflectiveness they bring to a task.

It was not long before her students adjusted to the closer examination of issues without feeling the need to move on.

THE EMERGENCE OF NEW CONTRIBUTORS

Traditionally 'successful' students can feel threatened by the emergence of other students in the new classroom dynamics of discussion. The encouraging nature of the community of inquiry certainly results in the emergence of previous non-contributors. Michael Whalley, an English philosopher, has looked at the reaction of traditionally successful students to the community of inquiry method:

> Students who are clever in the traditional academic sense are puzzled and resentful when they realise that philosophical questions are not amenable to simple, straightforward answers — even from the teacher. Such children have unfortunately been trained to perceive educational value only in what can be examined and tested. (Whalley 1989)

Some students find it hard to adjust to emphasis being placed on thinking about what others are saying, and the lack of appreciation of a hasty opinion. The fast respondents, and some teachers, are often intolerant of slower thinkers. One teacher's report included the following observations on this point :

> The material had an interesting effect on the usual distribution of ability and achievement in the class. Those students who were most confident and successful in the normal classes were not necessarily the most successful in this subject. This seemed to me to be partly because of the less goal-directed nature of the activity. Those children's success was often based on knowing what the goal was, and then heading for it regardless — in a sort of blinkered way.

When students are encouraged to look around at the general scenery, not just straight ahead, some are a little put out. On the other hand, other less successful students (less successful in the conventional classroom) make some outstanding contributions. Some are simply more able to see the interesting complexities that arise from a deeper examination of issues. Interestingly, too, the close examination of language enables the ESL students to make contributions, and join in in a way that is directly useful to them, and for their need for close language work.

Reviewing teaching styles

Through the development of a community of inquiry and involvement in a range of thinking activities, teaching styles change. Questioning and inquiry are promoted, logic and thinking skills are emphasised, and questions such as 'What if ...?', 'Is that a generalisation?' and 'Can you predict ...?', become common in discussions. The community of inquiry, with its challenging and encouraging mode, is a different way of operating.

One teacher reported that, following the development of a community of inquiry in her classroom, her students:
- were eager (sometimes almost too much so) to participate, the forest of hands presenting a welcome problem
- were disappointed when they missed out on being able to comment
- were able to recognise when a discussion had moved on, rendering further anecdotes inappropriate
- seemed proud of their ability to discuss important and difficult issues maturely

- were more prepared to listen to each other and value others' comments
- valued ideas more, moving well beyond the simple providing of examples or anecdotes

She also noted that:

- there was more evidence of students making comments such as 'John said ... but I think there is more to it than that.'
- they were trying to understand each other's meanings, sort out the various ideas they have heard, then make a contribution
- the students seemed to value discussion for its own sake, and did not insist on finding the right answer

Children are willing to listen to each other and value others' comments

STRATEGIES FOR BEGINNERS

As teachers, we often set the discussion agenda out of habit but the community of inquiry should be encouraging students' questions about stimulus materials. Students should be encouraged to say during a discussion when they don't understand a question or answer, or when they need something repeated for clarity or volume. The process of the discussion is an important aspect of the inquiry.

When forming a community of inquiry, try to avoid the following:

- over preparing

- being concerned with getting through the material rather than the quality of philosophical inquiry
- underestimating the intellectual abilities of students
- leading discussions as if you were taking an opinion poll: 'Justin, what do you think about that? That's interesting!' and 'What do you think, Jasmina? That's interesting too!'
- setting the discussion agenda

REVIEWING A DISCUSSION

It is not always necessary to summarise the achievements of a session or trace a conversation's drift. Particular conversational skills used, or thinking processes that occurred during a discussion, could be noted. An example would be: 'I think you used the concept of fairness well, and the examples you used were appropriate.' It is important that this does not result in the unnecessary repetition of the discussion. The benefit has already been achieved from involvement in the discussion and the skill acquisition may be very satisfactory, without needing to be spelt out.

The appropriate time for a discussion about skills or processes would be when a conversation did not build. An explanation of desired processes may then be in order. You could ask questions like:

'Was there another way we could have thought about that?'

or

'Did that discussion really help us understand our concerns?'

It does not take long for classes to recognise when they are being challenged by a philosophical conversation.

You could use the following checklist to examine discussion sessions:
- What's the issue or problem we are examining?
- What has been our focus?
- Are we giving reasons to support claims being made?
- Are we identifying assumptions if they are being made?
- Are implications of what's being said being explored?
- Are we testing the truth of what is being said, or asking how could we find out?
- Are examples of instances being given to support claims?

(Jackson 1989)

THE TEACHER'S ROLE

We often believe we (should) have most of the answers, and are used to having the students look to us as authority figures for those answers, but when involved in philosophical inquiry both teachers and students need to recognise there is not necessarily 'one' answer to issues they may be discussing.

Allowing the process of discovery to occur can be difficult to achieve. One teacher described her discussions as sometimes coming to a 'dead end'. When questioned further she said, 'The children don't seem to be able to see what I'm getting at.' After further discussion about the nature of dialogue in a community of inquiry she agreed there was nothing to fear in letting a conversation flow, aided when necessary by appropriate nudging by her, and using questions from appropriate exercises as a guide.

Her main concern was that she felt she too often injected her own point of view or judgement into the class discussion. Once she had practised the role of facilitator, rather than information giver, in a number of sessions, the balance shifted.

The community of inquiry gives teachers an opportunity to respond to students' verbal contributions differently. It is not necessary for the teacher's opinion to be known. With a bit of practice, we can change from the habit of saying after students' responses: 'Good', 'Yes' or 'Well done' to 'What do you think about what Alex said?', 'Who disagrees?' or 'That was one example, does anyone have another?'

Establishing a free-flowing philosophical conversation takes practice. It is all right to say 'I don't know, but let's find out.' Having 'the' answer and reaching a conclusion are not necessarily part of a philosophical conversation. Satisfaction is gained from the common enterprise.

CHANGES IN CLASSROOM DISCUSSIONS

One year 6 teacher reflected on changes to classroom discussions brought about by establishing a community of inquiry:

- The students are proud of their ability to discuss important and difficult issues maturely. They are more prepared to listen to each other and value others' comments. I cannot remember a case where a student was ridiculed for a comment.
- They also seem to value ideas more, moving well beyond the simple providing of examples or anecdotes.
- The students enjoy the challenge of the 'big questions and it is interesting that some of the less able (judged by writing skills) showed surprising ability in the explanation of complex ideas and concepts.
- There were times where there was a feeling in the air of students really stretching their thinking to find new ideas and possibilities.

- They have appreciated finding several approaches to an issue. They now understand concepts such as 'criteria' and the need to assess an issue from different perspectives.
- They are trying to understand each other's meanings, sort out the various ideas they have heard, then make a contribution.
- They seem to value discussion for its own sake, and do not insist on finding the right answer.
- The students are now confident with a sophisticated concept such as 'value'. It is unlikely that at this age they would have explored such a concept were it not for this program.
- Improvement in the area of thinking skills in the students handling of the rebuttal phase of a debate, e.g. responding to the logic of a previous speaker's comments.
- Students no longer accept that a proposition is right just because they say, believe, or feel it is.

When this class was asked what changes they had noticed they replied, 'Before we thought there was *an answer* to a question or issue, now we see there are angles. We're better at really listening. We try to sort out what someone else is saying, make sense of it and go on from there.'

ESL and NESB students and the community of inquiry

The following material has been adapted from a paper by Jackie Carroll, a Melbourne ESL teacher.

Teachers of students from non-English speaking backgrounds (NESB) who are learning English as a second language (ESL) are expressing interest in the community of inquiry procedure. The emphasis on oral language builds on the most natural way of learning a language — second language learning is most successful when there is immersion in the spoken language —and so there are many benefits from this method:

- The focus on dialogue is more inclusive of all students than traditional, didactic classrooms which focus on reading or writing.
- The content is relevant to all students because it is dictated by the students' interest, which means that students will be more encouraged to participate.
- It looks at the meanings of words at increasingly complex levels which helps students understand the English language better on a number of levels.
- The students are involved in more meaningful use of English than they might otherwise experience because topics such as 'What are

thoughts?', 'Are thoughts real?' and 'Why do we go to school?' have importance in their lives.

- Being engaged in philosophical discussions teaches students how to express opinions, agree or disagree with the opinions of others, clarify meaning, and give examples. It also provides the vocabulary they need to do this. These are precisely the sorts of skills, and the sort of vocabulary, that ESL students need in order to cope with the academic demands of schooling, and often the area in which they are least skilful.
- The methodology gives ESL students confidence in general (this is especially important for shy students), and confidence with using English in particular, when they see that they are able to have meaningful and complex discussions.
- Because of the curriculum emphasis on communication between students, ESL/NESB students get the opportunity to communicate with their native English-speaking peers and gain exposure to a number of different speaking models (not just the teacher).
- Students get to experiment with language as they study and learn it.
- Communication with native English-speaking peers increases social interaction among ethnic groups.

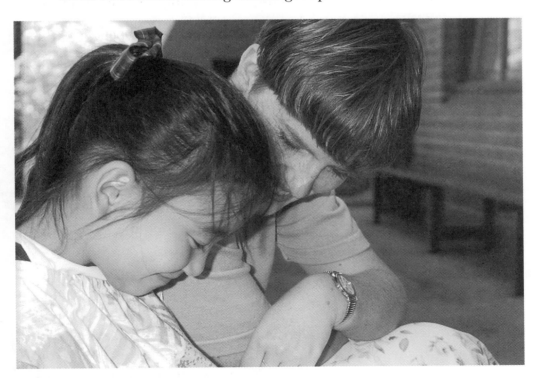

Students experiment with language, and learn together

STRATEGIES TO ENCOURAGE PARTICIPATION IN DISCUSSION

1 Pre-teach new vocabulary

It may be necessary to explain 'philosophical' vocabulary that might emerge in a discussion. Teachers could focus on the use of conventions such as agreeing, disagreeing, or asking for clarification prior to reading a text. Specific ways of asking for clarification such as 'Can you give an example?', 'What do you mean by that?' and 'Could you express that in a different way?' may need to be explained.

2 Use culturally specific resources

Resources which are highly specific to one culture can present a number of problems to ESL/NESB students (and even to native English speakers). Any colloquial language could be altered to plain English. Depending on the location, colloquial language such as *reckon*, *sidewalk*, or *frightfully*, should be explained, altered, or avoided altogether.

Some ideas contained in texts may be perceived differently by students from different ethnic backgrounds. For example, teachers should be aware of the cultural factors affecting individuals' beliefs, and ideas about such concepts as 'shame' and 'truth'. 'Shame', for example, has specific and varying cultural connotations of which the teacher may not be aware.

Other topics which may have different meanings among cultures are truth, goodness, the mind, death, crying, children's rights, freedom, duty, gift-giving, guests, friendship, art, and the nature of feelings. When discussing such concepts we need to anticipate cultural, as well as individual differences. The differences and similarities which arise are a philosophically rich potential resource.

3 Record discussion ideas

Some students, for a variety of reasons, have difficulty understanding the flow of the discussion. As the discussion progresses teachers could write the main ideas on the board. This can help those students who are aurally weak keep up with the discussion. Repetition helps to clarify the main ideas being discussed, the different ways of expressing the same ideas, as well as the new vocabulary being used.

4 Encourage clear expression

Encourage native speakers to express themselves as clearly as possible. If some students have difficulty understanding contributions of native-speaking students, ask the student involved to repeat what they said in another way. If the student cannot clarify their statement, ask the other students to try. This will help all students to communicate more clearly.

5 Recap discussions

A brief recap of the discussion will help students consolidate what they have heard. Look at:

- the main ideas that were discussed
- different ways each idea was discussed
- new vocabulary

(Some teachers prefer not to use this technique as they feel it takes away from the freshness of a discussion.)

6 Set written tasks

Because the main focus is on discussions, students are not normally asked to complete writing tasks. Writing, as one of the four macro-skills, forms an integral part of the language lesson for ESL students, and neglecting this skill may have a negative affect on the other three skills: speaking, listening and reading. We need to devise writing tasks that will revise, and reinforce, philosophical concepts and new vocabulary.

Students could be asked to write about a question they found interesting, mentioning the various ways it may be considered. Or they could be asked to defend or refute a certain viewpoint. It is not necessary to be didactic in assigning the writing task. Indeed, it is preferable if students write from their own interest, just as the discussion arises out of students' interest. However, you may want to specify items to be included in the written work which you feel need attention. Five to ten minutes could be assigned at the end of a session for journal entries.

7 Monitor progress

One useful feature of written work is that it allows the teacher to more closely monitor student progress. Setting written work is one way to check whether students understand the philosophical concepts and are internalising the vocabulary.

Examples of students' written work can be used to provide useful models of what is required in written tasks. The examples could be placed on an overhead projector or copies handed out to the class.

8 Consult with ESL staff

Teachers should consult with ESL staff in their schools if they have any questions about the suitability of any activities or sections of a story, or to discuss difficulties they are not sure how to handle. Asking them to participate in discussion sessions is one way to get advice. Getting ESL staff involved in a community of inquiry program would be even better.

CHAPTER THREE

Case Studies Demonstrating Communities of Inquiry

This chapter contains case studies of teachers' experiences using the philosophical inquiry approach. It begins with some general guidelines.

Tips for beginners

The need for introductory activities prior to more sustained text examination has been discussed in Chapter 2. The benefits of such activities are that they stimulate the asking of challenging questions and the development of listening, thinking and discussion skills.

By working with a range of thinking activities which concentrate on abstract concepts and philosophical issues, you will find that your teaching style will change to incorporate the practice of questioning and promoting inquiry, logic and a range of thinking skills. Using questions like 'What if ...?, 'Is that a generalisation?' or 'Can you expand on that?' will become commonplace. The community of inquiry, with its challenging and encouraging mode, is a different way of operating which both your and your class will enjoy.

- **Ensure that you are familiar with the issues** contained in the stimulus material and any accompanying exercises before you begin work.

- **Have a few relevant questions on hand** (perhaps ready on your lap) to inject into your classroom discussion. This is a core requirement to ensure your discussions will develop. Using good philosophical questions helps you to probe deeper into issues.

- **Encourage more verbal interaction** between your class members, rather than a teacher/child/teacher pattern. For example, questions like:
  'How does that compare with what Eli said?'

'Can you add to Sam's point?'
'Are you agreeing with Chris?'
'Could you perhaps ask Kim to say it another way?'
Responses like the following move the discussion back to the class rather than into the teacher's domain.
'Give an example to help us understand your point.'
'What if I were to say [provide a counter-argument]. Would you still say that?'
'What have we found out about that, Mira?'
'Let me know later if you change your mind after hearing others' opinions.'

- **Keep notes** on sessions and preparation. This cuts down preparation for future sessions.

- **Use a variety of ways of recording** student questions. For example: overhead projectors, chalk- and white-boards, let students write up the questions, have groups work together to list questions on butchers paper.

- **Vary the source material**. Films, newspaper articles, extracts from movies, and, of course, a host of literature will provide a wide variety of issues.

- **Don't allow a discussion to drag** out for too long. For example, when students offer a series of anecdotes around one point (my dog does *x*, my dog does *x* etc.) the discussion is not progressing.

- **Emphasise key issues** or words discussed in class (e.g. by writing them on the board).

- To cope with large numbers, **divide your class into groups**. For example, set one group to work on exercises associated with the discussion topic that can be answered in written form, or suggest they illustrate part of a story. This leaves you free to have a discussion with a smaller group. Try the following variations:
  - a group of good contributors, perhaps not great listeners
  - a group of reluctant contributors, probably good listeners

- **Remember to wait** a little longer for an answer or contribution from the thinkers who take longer to formulate a response. Their contributions will be worth waiting for. View silences as positive thinking times.

How to recognise philosophical discussion

One answer that could be given is that you can 'feel' that it is different. To begin with, your thinking and the students' thinking is noticeably challenged — creative and critical approaches are emerging as you raise new topics. The discussions attend to issues that are often abstract, and that have no (if any) straightforward answer.

Here are some questions you could ask to test whether some of the key elements of a philosophical discussion are present:

- Were the participants (including the teacher) listening to one another?
- Were the participants responding directly to one another?
- Were people encouraged to participate?
- Did the discussion 'scratch beneath the surface'?
- Was the topic interesting?
- Did I challenge my own thinking?

(Jackson 1989)

Most teachers evaluate sessions with their class using questions like these. Together they might decide what they would like to alter about the discussion format next session, or identify how they might improve their discussion.

The case studies

The following case studies examine the work of teachers from a range of year levels as they developed and discovered the features of a community of inquiry. Their session planning, student and self- evaluation and resources worked with should provide guidelines for others. **Although specific classes are described, the issues and resources apply to a broad range of year levels**. They provide examples of how teachers and their classes worked to improve their communities of inquiry, including:

- asking questions to enhance discussion
- checklists for assessing whether philosophy is occurring
- classroom activities resulting from using a variety of resources
- examples of critical and creative thinking

Some transcripts have been included to demonstrate a variety of discussion styles and to highlight some pitfalls.

Choosing resources
Andy's year 6

Following early sessions which established a nurturing community of inquiry, Andy introduced the broad topic of 'rights' by using the following resources.

1 **A newspaper article** about censorship led to a discussion about whether anyone should have the right to restrict our attendance at movies or access to videotapes. As the issues was of interest to the class, they wanted to contribute. Andy noted their questions about the topic for further discussion.

    She constantly reminded the class about features of a good discussion by encouraging students to listen, think about the issue and address each other directly. During discussions her typical contributions were: 'Hands up (or down)', 'One at a time', 'Listen carefully to what Sal is saying', 'Do you agree with Pat or Jules?' and 'Respond directly to Ming, not me, please'.

    She used 'prompt' questions about rights from a text containing philosophical issues when she felt the discussion needed enrichment. For example:

    - 'Does censorship of X-rated movies take away or add to our rights?'
    - 'In what instances might it be right to remove someone's rights?' (Note the two meanings of 'right', which would need to be defined before discussion.)
    - 'Who decides the rights of (a) children, and (b) adults? Are they the same?'
    - 'Does a right guarantee anything?'

2 A videotaped **documentary** featuring a woman revisiting the scene of a crocodile attack on her raised questions about the issue of animal rights and the environment.
    - 'Do you think that animals killing out of instinct should be killed? Is there a difference if a human is the prey?'
    - 'In what instances is it okay to kill an animal? Does the same apply to humans?'
    - 'What is meant by respect for territory? How do we decide who should have rights in a particular place?'

3 **Short stories and anecdotes** provided another rich source of material. Andy used the following short segment which contains issues of fairness, pride, unfair reprimands, non-verbal actions and teasing.

A Melbourne school was hosting a group of visiting Thai students for a day. During one session in a year 5 class, the visitors were asked to join students in groups to talk about their country. One group asked their visitor how to say a particular swear word in Thai. After being told how to pronounce this word by the visitor, they began to practise saying it over and over, laughing as each said it louder that before.   At the recess break, the visitors went out to play with the class.Someone yelled the well-practised swear word at one of the visitors.

He said nothing, but hid in the schoolyard and did not return to class at the end of the break. When the visitors were due to leave, the cause for the visitor's disappearance was discovered.

The next day the year 5 teacher told the class they were banned from attending their week at camp. Two students who had not been involved in the swearing incident walked out of class in silent protest. Their teacher said nothing as they walked past her and out into the yard.

Andy recognised the importance of allowing the students to choose the issues for discussion. She wrote the questions students asked about the passage using an overhead projector and put their names in brackets at the end of their question.

- 'Why didn't the teacher yell at the students when they walked out?' (Pete)
- 'Was the punishment of the whole class fair?' (Dana)
- 'Was it racism or just having fun?' (Lew)
- 'If the swear word had been in English would it have ended up the same?' (Rav)

Andy used the community of inquiry approach for the heated discussion that followed. At times, when it appeared everyone wanted to speak at once, she suggested the students discuss the question in pairs for a while and then report back.

4 **Novels** can be a great source of issues. From a discussion about chapter 6 of Natalie Babbit's book *Tuck Everlasting*, Andy elicited from the class the following issues and questions:

- 'Can you call what Mae Tuck is doing kidnapping? '
- 'Why do people kidnap?'
- 'Why didn't she call out to the person in the yellow suit?'
- 'Why is Winnie confused/frightened? Should you trust strangers?'
- 'Why didn't she struggle/object?'
- 'Why do people try to remember their past?'
- 'Is kidnapping the answer to all problems?'

She divided the points raised by the class into questions about the story and questions about the issues. This demonstrated to the students which issues had potential (philosophically) and which were more like a 'normal' English classroom discussion.

Andy noted the way the class began to brush aside, or handle quickly, the more straightforward questions in favor of discussions of the more philosophical topics. Questions like 'When do we do our best thinking?' and 'Is it really a kidnapping?', which led to the issue of freedom, were dealt with in a lively, philosophical discussion to which almost all the class contributed. Planned follow-up exercises included questions which further probed the meaning and implications of the word 'freedom'.

After a semester's work Andy wrote the following report about these sessions:

> Students were eager ... to participate, the forest of hands presenting a welcome problem. There was disappointment when they missed out on being able to comment. Some students were annoyed when they wanted to contribute, but found that by the time they were asked to contribute, the discussion had moved beyond their point, rendering it inappropriate.
>
> They seem proud of their ability to discuss important and difficult issues maturely. They are more prepared to listen to each other and value others' comments ...
>
> Students value *ideas* more, moving well beyond the simple providing of examples or anecdotes. There is more evidence of comments such as 'John said ... but I think there is more to it than that.'
>
> They are trying to understand each other's meanings, sort out the various ideas they have heard, then make a contribution. They value discussion for its own sake, and do not insist on finding *the* right answer.

Focusing on the evidence
Adam's Year 5

Adam commented on the way his students were responding to the logic (or lack of logic) of others' comments. He had noticed students no longer felt that a belief was sufficient for the acceptance of a proposition. Students in the class commented:

> *'Before we thought there must be* an answer *to a question or issue, now we see there are many angles to most things we discuss.'*

> *'We're better at really listening. We try to sort out what someone else is saying, make sense of it and go on from there.'*

After his class had been using community of inquiry methods for about a year, Adam felt a couple of students were almost sabotaging discussions with 'super-lateral thoughts' and nonsensical comments. They had become adept at introducing other possible worlds with their unlimited scope.

He used a reasoning exercise, asking the class to identify whether either of the following were examples of good reasoning.

a. All possums are mammals.

All possums are bushy-tailed.

Therefore, all mammals are bushy-tailed.

b. All rodents are animals.

All rats are rodents.

Therefore, all rats are animals.

Even though time had been spent at the beginning of the session talking about only using the available information, students said statement one was wrong because there are possums which are not bushy-tailed. They were brought back to the two given statements for consideration. They found it quite difficult to, firstly, take the sentences as true (for the purposes of the exercise), and, secondly, not add information they knew about the various animals mentioned.

The rules had to be restated many times as students kept giving counter-instances (appropriate at other times). Finally, about one-third of the class was able to deduce whether the conclusions were true based on the evidence.

Adam observed that the discussion skills developed in these sessions had transferred to students' discussion of literature generally. He noted the following changes in the class's approach to discussions:

> . . . the students are enjoying the challenge that the 'big' issues

provide ... some of the less able writers are demonstrating the ability to explain complex concepts verbally ... the class is finding new possibilities and ideas by stretching their thinking ... they appreciate using several approaches to one issue and the need to assess an issue from different perspectives ... they are able to discuss sophisticated concepts such as 'fairness', 'criteria', 'evidence', and 'value'.

Philosophy.

Georgina Hoad

I think there are more than three meanings to belonging or belongings; for example the belonging to a group and the belonging to a table like a leg and the belongings as in property, and the belonging like a page to a book which belongs to me. In the last one the page belongs to the book as in a group or property because the page is in a group of pages which belong to the book and or the way the page belongs to the book so it is the book's property and the book can belong to me.

Encouraging students' reflective thinking
Pam's Year 4

Pam felt that her discussions were deteriorating too often into mere anecdotal points around the same point. For example, when discussing whether both humans and animals 'hope', the following dialogue developed.

> *Charlotte: I know my dog hopes because he sits at the door waiting for dinner.*
> *Rafiq: My dog hopes I'll give him his dinner when I get the plate.*
> *Maria: My cat hopes because she sits by her bowl ...*

In this case, the point of the discussion was to ascertain the students' understanding of similarities and differences between animals and humans. 'Hope' was merely one point. Moving on to discussion, another characteristic, for example 'cry', would get the discussion 'unstuck'. A discussion can also be moved on by asking for an evaluation of one student's point:

> *'Mike, what do you think about Raf's point? Is that an example of an animal hoping?'*

Having prepared questions about the issue can also help you to move the discussion on. As the facilitator of the discussion, you need to keep your overall aims in mind and take responsibility for the standard of discussion. Being a silent observer is rarely sufficient.

Students can be kept on track by asking them to identify the point to which they are responding. Questions are a great way of moving on:

> *'Are you responding to what Dan just said, Lim, or is that point connected with something said some time ago?'*

Pam was wanting to be less vocal in her classroom discussions, while still being and effective facilitator. She wanted the students to respond to each other and break away from the teacher/student/teacher/student pattern of response. The following extracts from classroom discussions contain reminders for us all. (T = teacher, S = student)

1 When the teacher wants a certain answer

Although we may not realise it, very often, even if we have said we are interested in promoting the students' opinions, we will steer a discussion towards our own end point. The following extract of dialogue speaks for itself:

> T: Talk about it? Think about it? Or do you think they would just

walk past it and forget it? Hari, what do you think?

S: Um. (*silence*)

T: Have a guess, it doesn't matter what you say. Do you think that people would be interested in it as they walk through, or do you think they would just walk past it?

S: Walk past.

T: Why do you feel that. I'm going to force you a little now.

S: They are not really interested in it.

T: But ... but ... can someone give me another opinion and tell me why they might be interested in it?

S: It's controversial.

T: Excellent, it is controversial.

2 When the students respond to one another:

The students are discussing censorship. The teacher has learned to step back and listen to the students discuss an issue. This extract also demonstrates the teacher asking the students questions which require elaboration. The teacher is interested in hearing the students' opinions. The students are responding directly to each other, and the teacher encourages this by her questioning.

T: Then why do they have [censors' ratings] guidelines? Have they been imposed for a reason?

S: It should be a person's choice.

S: I think ratings like M's and R's they should just put recommendations, but if the children really want to see it then they should be allowed to.

S: I don't agree with that, because some younger boys will want to go to see something like *The Terminator* and I don't think younger children should see violence like that. It's been shown in studies that it does affect them.

S: Yes, they're not mature enough.

S: (*the previous speaker continues*) Like those two little kids who kidnapped and killed that boy in England.

S: I could go either way with that because there's a pretty good argument on both sides, like freedom of choice which says whatever you want to do should be allowed, and then the other is that you have to protect people from violence in a movie, because as you said, little kids get influenced by what they see.

T: So, are they two opposing arguments?

S: You can't agree or disagree because they both are important.

S: Getting back to art. With art, you can interpret it the way you want to interpret it, but with a movie it sort of sends you one way or another. You can't really go to a film like *Natural Born Killers* and say it was really artistic. I haven't seen it but say if they were killing each other you would have to say he is killing someone, while in art you can say I can interpret it this way.

T: So you think it's more open to interpretation?

S: I don't think you can talk about film and art in this way, because when you are 11 or 12 you are not really interested in going to an art exhibition, so they're not going to see something like the AIDS exhibition. But once you are older and are interested in going to an exhibition, then you can make your own choice. Do you see what I mean?

The student's question here is an important feature of good inquiry. It demonstrates her involvement and, points to the discussion being 'owned' by the students.

Students respond to one another during discussion

3. When the teacher repeats what students say

How often do we do this? The habit of repeating what a student has said, and then elaborating on their point can be easily overcome by asking the student to elaborate. Otherwise sessions may sound like this:

S: What they smelt like.

T: What they smelt like. So you can imagine what they smelt like?

S: What sound it made.

T: The sounds it made. So you could imagine it shouting or creaking or groaning slobbering or whatever, remember that character in *Lord of the Rings* that cat/monkey creature that slithered and hissed its way around for the precious ring. (*Hand goes up*) Yes?

S: How it felt.

T: How it felt. Whether it was icy cold. Icy cold, that would be nice on a day like this wouldn't it. Icy cold. So really we had you go into that world through your senses. Now I'm going to ask you something today that is a bit different and that's why I'm talking this way about the senses. I'm going to ask you to imagine something. You're going to see it in your head like that TV screen up there, and you're going to see something in your head, each of you with a slightly different view than what it really is. It's something I know, and you're going to see it by the words that I give you and then I'm going to ask you some questions about it.

4. When undeserved praise is given

We are sometimes overzealous with our praise. The comments made by the students in the following extract are fairly ordinary and should have been responded to in kind. There are other ways of encouraging good contributions, preferably after something terrific has been said. We should, however, aim to assist our students to have the confidence to contribute without looking for our approval. It is obvious from this extract that the students in this class may not develop this confidence because it appears the teacher is after particular answers.

T: A person who deals in what sort of cars?

S: Classic cars.

T: Very good. So, a car expert is a connoisseur, a vintage car connoisseur. What other sort of connoisseur could you have?

S: A judge, perhaps.

T: A judge, and what would he be connoisseur of?

S: Cats or dogs.

T: Very clever, geez, I didn't think of that one either. You are very good. That's where you surprised me the other day. Your imagination is wonderful, you can really come up with some good solutions. Someone who can judge something like a cat and dog show, at the Royal Show or something like that. What else? (*Indicates to student with hand up*). All right Theo what do you think?

S: A surfer watching a wave.

T: A surfer watching a wave. Isn't that a good idea? One last one.

S: Wine.

T. Wine. I hoped someone would say this. I mentioned this person in the sculpture liked drinking a little bit and eating a lot, and I sort of hoped you would bring the two together.

5. When the teacher interrupts

It is not only the students who need to learn to listen to contributions during a discussion, as this extract shows:

T. But, now they use these things, they drive cars etc.

S. Yeah, but ...

T. But this is still ... remember their dreamings are still very important and they still use styrene cups and hog hair brushes.

S. I think it's the same. Just because they have used different materials it doesn't mean the work they are trying to reproduce is not the same.

T. Is this a sign of the times that progress ...

S. Say if Michelangelo used crayons instead of paint, that would still be ...(*teacher interrupts*)

T. He would still use better paints probably than what he did?

S. Yeah, exactly, he...(*teacher interrupts*)

T. Would that still be the same work?

By using 'but' the teacher can be seen to be either after a particular answer from the students, or trying to drive her own point home. Interrupting a student before they have finished speaking is difficult to justify.

Session planning
Dia's Year 3

The notes below illustrate how Dia planned and evaluated her early sessions. She kept a diary of session content, and had a colleague take specific observations about her sessions.

SESSION ONE

Planning

The class was to read part of a story about a child in a pool — imagining that she is a fish and thinking about the distortions of sound and vision caused by being underwater. There was so much discussion potential that I doubted we would have time to do any written work. However, if restlessness set in, I had prepared an exercise which followed up the parts of the story where states of matter are mentioned: 'Are the following liquid, gas or a solid: a table, your eyes, a cloud, your teeth, a river, a balloon?' (Based on Lipman 1986)

After reading, the class asked questions about most of the issues the story contained. We wrote them on the board with the students' names beside them ready for discussion.

I had another teacher note which children answered questions or had their hand up wanting to respond. This gave me a good indication of individuals' participation. I was trying to include the more reluctant contributors by asking them specific questions, and was pleased with many individuals' progress in oral contributions.

A few items of discussion were left for the beginning of the next session, when I would refer to my list and make sure I included the students who had not contributed this session.

SESSION TWO

Discussion

Another teacher took notes during the discussion session. The following is an example of one question and answer segment. (Student responses follow the question originally asked by the students.)

Q: What is meant by 'Steam is water, water is water'?

'It's steam if the water gets too hot and it kind of evaporates into the air. Evaporation looks misty.'

'Steam is when hot air catches in cold air, the hot water is coming into the cold air. Ice is real frozen water.'

'You can make the water frozen by putting it into the freezer. It gets larger if you put it in the cup in the freezer for a long time. The water gets larger and   cracks the glass.'

'I disagree — you might have a plastic cup. Another word for getting larger is expanding.'

'Sound can hit something and can be amplified by a certain kind of thing.'

Students are encouraged to respond to each other

Evaluation

I was thrilled with the discussion. We covered the chalkboard with vocabulary the children used. The class was extremely interested in the text and follow-up discussion was enjoyable.

They are starting to respond to one another. I find if I say nothing, but point to another child for the next comment, they will respond to this and not expect my approval.

The scientific discussion that emerged about states of matter reminded us how important it is to define terms precisely. Before we started, we talked about examples of solid, liquid and gas, but when we began classifying things like eyes (spongy, etc.), students found it harder to make firm rules, and more vocabulary and new concepts emerged.

Dia took more than one inquiry session a week. One was formally time-tabled, the others arose incidentally either out of other class work or when she found a few spare minutes in a day. In a report at the end of the first year she described changes she had observed in her teaching method and in the students' participation.

> There has been a definite change in the way I hold a class discussion ... I don't make as many comments on the class's opinions, (i.e. always think my viewpoint takes priority over theirs) ...
>
> I allow others to support what has been said or refute it. I won't accept mere 'Yes' or 'No' or 'I don't know' answers as readily as I did and most times insist on asking 'Why do you think that?' or 'Can you give me an example to support that?'
>
> We have been able to encourage some of the less confident class members to participate and make them aware that they have a worthwhile opinion of their own, not necessarily a right or wrong one, with a right or wrong answer. This has been a big change as the class has come to realise that there is not always the answer, their own answers need to be backed up, or can be changed.

In a classroom we don't always get the time to really talk and listen to one another. One change Dia noticed was her students listening directly to each other. She was no longer filtering all conversations and this was no longer expected. Another change she noticed was that, whereas the class had previously tended to concentrate on real life situations when having a discussion, abstract concepts were now prominent. The experience in philosophical inquiry changed her approaches to discussions across the curriculum.

Developing the issues
Chris's Year 2

Observing Chris taking an early session reminded me of the importance of thorough preparation. He had not been using philosophical inquiry for long and was aiming to conduct a philosophically rich discussion from questions the class raised about a story they had read. (Lipman 1988, p.13) Unfortunately, the students tended to merely repeat statements from the extract, and Chris did not encourage students to formulate these statements into questions. He admitted after the session that he did not believe his students could formulate ideas into questions. Examples of statements students made were:

> *'She didn't wait to see how other people ate bananas.'*
> *'She doesn't have any manners.'*
> *'She left her looks and manners at home.'*
> *'She started to eat a cake.'*
> *'She thinks she does everything wrong.'*

I reminded the class that we did not want re-statements of the story, like the cake statement above, but issues they'd like to talk about further. They then contributed: 'What does it mean to have manners?'

> *'Is Bella right when she says she does everything wrong?'*
> *'Why does she feel like that?'*

When Chris encouraged the students to say what they thought about this point, one said:

> *'She only thinks about what she does wrong.'*

Chris wasn't sure how to develop this point as he had not thought through the philosophical issues contained in the story, nor had he read the exercises written to accompany the story. One exercise, for example, examined the words 'good/bad' and 'right/wrong' and aimed to draw out whether meanings have moral connotations or practical aspects. For example:

- What makes someone a bad person?
- What actions might a good person perform?
- How can good and bad actions affect others?

Had he prepared more thoroughly, he would have been able to facilitate more valuable discussion.

It is important, especially in the early stages of developing a community of inquiry, to use resources that have been written to aid the introduction of philosophical inquiry. Some examples of these are provided in Chapter 5. It is important to be familiar with the philosophical content of stories and to approach it with understanding. A knowledge of the content of an exercise, and how it might by used during a session, is almost a prerequisite for profitable discussion.

Creative and rigorous thinking on chosen topics
Dino's Year 3

Dino asked me to observe one of his sessions because he was excited about the creative thinking his class was demonstrating. In the class I observed he used an exercise to follow up the question 'What is a word?' raised by a student in a previous session. (Lipman 1986, p. 196) A transcript of the questions asked, and the students' creative responses, follows:

Q: Can words be danced?(sung? spoken? read? thought?)
Responses:
'You can make up a dance to express words.'
'You can do all those things.'
'When you write things the pen could be dancing over the page.'
'There are no words, but ballets dance a story, e.g. Beauty and the Beast.'
'Miming is like dancing — you're making words by actions, you mime to the words.'
'Mr Elias dances the words when he takes poetry.'
'When you say words like 'because' the vibrations dance in the air when you speak.'
'You could have a big sign with independent letters and make it dance.'
'Words can't be thought if you mean you see them like a sign in your head.'
'You could write the letter 'e' on the floor and we could dance it on the floor.'

Q: Can words have no meaning at all?
Responses:
'Yes, a wrongly spelt word.'
'You could make up a word.'
'You can make up a word that means something to you only.'
'Another language.'
'Computers have different languages, some won't mean anything to other systems.'

Q: Can you hurt a person with a word?
Responses:
'Yes, a swear word will hurt feelings.'
'You can't hurt a tough kid with words that might hurt others.'

'You can hurt yourself with words — the reaction of someone you insult, e.g. being hit for saying "You stink!"'

'It depends on how someone will react to words.'

'You could hurt a cripple by saying, "I'll race you 50 metres" — he couldn't do it.'

The class discussed each question productively and creatively in a session that lasted for nearly an hour.

Dino was aware of changes in his discussion technique — his new found ability to extend ideas, propose situations, to stimulate and test the class's ability to judge, reason, etc. He had begun to rarely judge responses by saying 'Very good, Van' or 'Right', but rather deflected responses to others in the group by asking questions like 'What do other people think?' or 'Can anyone think of a time when this might not be true?'. This technique is effective in helping students develop the confidence to contribute without needing affirmation from the teacher.

Apart from encouraging the students to listen, reason and assess a situation, Dino noted that working out reasons why was proving to be most beneficial in other areas of the curriculum such as social and religious studies.

Journey   Katherine.
                                                      1·4·95

The word journey can be used in many different ways. A journey can be travelling through time, physical or mental or to go on a trip. Your journey can continue through other people's minds besides your own. Another way of going on a journey is by imagining or dreaming. Journeys can have limits but you make them yourself.

That is my description of Journey

Planning for good questioning
Sal's Year 4

Sal had working with philosophy for some time but felt she was in need of some help with planning to use good questions. She planned five discussion possibilities around a story. (Lipman 1986, p. 36) The topics which were discussed demonstrated the maturity level of the class by the end of their second year of doing philosophy. They were nine or ten years old.

PLANNING: POSSIBLE ISSUES FOR DISCUSSION

1 Turtle - Hurting animals
   Some people harm harmless animals.
   When might it be okay to hurt/kill an animal?

2 The word 'like'
   three meanings: similar to, an example, admire/prefer

3 Hypothesising
   Tom formulates a hypothesis — what is the evidence? Counter-argument?
   NB Interesting — Tom alleges non-existent things are capable of having negative weight.

4 Are there ghosts?
   Criteria for existence? e.g. must it have weight? (refuted by objects in outer space)

5 'It's stupid to be afraid of something that doesn't exist.'
   Can you be afraid of nothing? Difference between 'is afraid of nothing' and 'is not afraid of anything.'
6 Can hands think?
   Examples?

THE SESSION

The class read the story, and the students raised the following points for discussion.

'Why throw rocks at the turtle? What's he doing to you?' (Cathy)
'Why didn't he admit he was scared?' (Tran)
'Does a ghost weigh anything? Do they exist?' (Pia)
'His hands sweated and he didn t understand it.' (Jorge)

A visiting teacher took the following notes of the questions Sal used during the session, as Sal wanted to check on her questioning techniques. She was pleased with the way her students were raising issues, but felt the conversation sometimes 'drifted' too much for her liking. This session, she had questions about the story, and associated questions her students had already raised, in her lap ready to inject when needed. During a 45-minute session she asked the following questions:

> 'Does what happened in the story happen in real life?'
> 'Is killing animals the same kind of thing as throwing stones at a turtle?'
> 'Now responding to what he has said, is that a reason for killing animals?'
> 'Why didn't Kio admit he was scared?'
> 'Why wouldn't you admit that you are scared, Sam? Does it matter what other people think?'
> 'What would happen if Sam admits he's scared? Might the others all admit it too?'
> 'What the children in the story are doing is hypothesising. Do you know what that is?'
> 'Susan, what is Tom saying in favor of his theory?'
> 'Is there enough evidence to say there is a ghost?'
> 'What does it mean to exist?'
> 'Shari, is shuffling and moaning evidence for something existing, like Pia said?'
> 'Does something have to have weight to exist?'
> 'What about an idea? Does that exist?'
> 'Have people's comments made anyone change their mind? Bobbie?'
> 'Is air the same thing as an idea?'
> 'In space, is there still weight?'
> 'If there were ghosts, would they have to weigh something?'
> 'Is he saying he can't control his sweating and that it means he's scared?'
> 'Freda, can you be afraid of something that doesn't exist? Of nothing if it doesn't exist?'
> 'Is there a difference between "Is afraid of nothing" and "Not afraid of anything"?'

Sal was pleased with the session content. She felt her questioning was good and was pleased to note she was starting to encourage students to respond to each other. Her aim was to inject more inclusive questions like these in future sessions, and to further encourage students to build on each other's comments. The session demonstrated the extent to which children can be philosophically challenged. When the class was asked why they thought they were working in this way, their replies reflected Sal's aims:

- to have discussions about things
- to think about problems
- to be able to look at something in different ways
- so that we can join in the conversation
- so that we can think for ourselves
- we don't just say any old thing, we think before we say it
- we find out what things are about
- to have fun
- to listen to others and what they say
- we can have an opinion
- so we might change our mind if we want to
- we think about further conversation
- to get ideas from others

Good questioning leads to good discussion

Monitoring Progress

Six methods of testing discussions

The following methods are examples teachers and researchers have used to test whether the skills of philosophical inquiry are present in a discussion.

1 The use of checklists to determine whether the key elements of a philosophical discussion are present.

2 A report system, developed in an Australian school, which lists skills and attitudes appropriate for testing philosophical dispositions.

3 Two examples of teachers monitoring student contributions during a class.

4 Matthew Lipman's suggested evaluation of student progress.

5 Research conducted in Mexico in which non-classroom conversations of children were recorded to ascertain whether there was a carry-over of skills from classroom philosophy sessions.

6 A selection of anecdotal reflections of a group of primary teachers using philosophy.

1 CHECKLISTS

The following questions are a useful starting point in identifying a good discussion:

• Were the participants listening to one another?
• Were the participants responding to one another?
• Did most people participate, or just a few dominators?
• Did our discussion 'scratch beneath the surface' and 'open up' the topic?
• Was the topic interesting?
• Did I challenge my own thinking?

Teachers and students can usually 'feel' that something different is happening in their minds as they work hard at discussing issues, matters of logic, etc. It is as though a new part of the brain is operating.

2 REPORTS

The following report format reflects the skills being developed in a community of inquiry. It was developed by teachers who had worked with philosophical inquiry for a number of years and devised so that parents could see the development of particular skills of dialogue in their child. The report gave equal weighting to

- internal conceptual skills (such as those of logical reasoning)
- skills that reflected principles of clear reasoning (such as the ability to provide relevant examples)
- skills that reflected the quality of the interaction between a particular student and their peers, such as the ability to consider another's point of view (Glaser 1989)

The report forms were then made available for other teachers. They help monitor whether individual students are developing the requisite skills and dispositions.

SKILLS	Comments: yes/no

Skills of inquiry
    Asks relevant questions
    Shows sensitivity to context in discussion
    Demonstrates ability to find relevant examples
    Shows openness to new ideas
 	
Skills of logical reasoning
    Displays consistency when developing a point of view
    Able to express ideas coherently
 	
Skills of dialogue
    Able to paraphrase another's ideas
    Able to build upon another's ideas
    Discusses issues with objectivity
    Able to listen attentively
    Accepts corrections by peers willingly
 	
Attitude
    Shows respect for members of the community of inquiry
    Is willing to persevere and attempt tasks set in a positive way	

The second report was designed for secondary classes, but many of the checks are relevant for primary students.

SKILLS	Comments: yes/no

Skills of inquiry
    Able to discuss issues with objectivity
    Asks relevant questions
    Shows sensitivity to context in discussion
    Understands the need for supporting
    opinion with reasons
    Demonstrates ability to find relevant
    examples
    Shows openness to new ideas
 	
Skills of logical reasoning
    Capable of detecting underlying assumptions
    Able to distinguish between definitions and
    examples
    Displays consistency when developing a point
    of view
 	
Skills of dialogue
    Able to build upon another's ideas
    Discusses issues with objectivity
    Able to take another's ideas seriously
    Accepts corrections by peers willingly
 	
  Behavior
    Shows respect for people in the community
    of inquiry
    Works well in small groups
    Works well independently
    Is a cooperative, sensible and courteous
    member of class	

3 MONITORING CONTRIBUTIONS

The following are examples of evaluations by teachers in Melbourne primary schools. The first is an assessment of student progress after having conducted philosophy classes once a week for about four months. For example:

Lachie: Has contributed well since the program began.
Min: Paying better attention during discussions.
Evan: Increased contribution to discussions, but sometimes 'silly'.
Sim: Only offers input if asked, but answers show her to be involved.
Tom: Began very indifferently, now contributes well.

The second is part of a count of student answers offered during one session. The teacher was interested to check who was contributing, so he had another teacher monitor student input.

Amber ////	*Very good level of response. Normally needs to be called upon.*
Bennie /////	*Very good. Normally little or no response.*
Bang Le /	*Normally contributes a lot, but not a great thinker.*
Herta ////	*Very pleasing, because his input is normally 'immature'.*

Each method was useful. The monitored participation allowed the teachers to gain a clearer idea of what was happening during discussions, and to concentrate attention on particular students. Subsequent monitoring showed improved participation in each case

4 EVALUATION OF STUDENT PROGRESS

In one of his manuals Matthew Lipman has provided an evaluation checklist which teachers at any year level might find useful (Lipman 1980). It includes general questions for teachers to ask themselves about student progress, for example:

1 Can each student distinguish between a reason and a good reason? How do I know? Are they manifesting this skill in the way they speak to one another?

2 Do the students ask appropriate questions of one another during discussions? For example 'Why do you say that?'

3 Are the more non-verbal students participating more? Am I doing everything I can to encourage them?

There are also spaces for teachers to provide student names under statements like the following:

1 Students who directed remarks to other students many times while doing this chapter.

2 Students who are regularly giving reasons for their views during discussions.

3 Students who are still silent during discussions.

4 Students who are not giving reasons for their views during discussions.

5 Students who need teacher encouragement to elaborate on their ideas, especially in terms of what follows from what they are saying:

Keeping records

If specific skills taught and others to be further worked on are identified, it is a good idea to keep a record of them. Recording exercises that worked and why, and noting literature, video or film that relates to particular themes, provides a useful resource for later sessions.

5 RECORDING NON-CLASSROOM CONVERSATIONS

Eugenio Echeverria, the director of Guadalajara Centre for Philosophy for Children in Mexico, tried to establish to what extent the conversational and thinking skills developed in philosophy sessions transfer into the areas of the curriculum and children's talk. He listened to, and recorded, the conversations of two young people (ages not specified) for a year — both in the playground and in the lunchroom — to ascertain whether there were perceivable changes in their dialogue and whether discussion topics raised in the class survived into schoolground discussions. The questions being researched were:

1 Are the skills learned via philosophy for children applied by the students?
2 Where does the application of the skills take place?
3 What is the nature of this application?

While he did not believe that one conversation would provide a true impression, grouping conversations together might. He described his testing as qualitative, with guiding questions and assertions supported by anecdotes. By the end of the year, 440 interactions had been identified and recorded. They were classified as follows:

Thinking skills	Settings
Detection of underlying assumptions Identification of contradictory statements Provision of reasons Provision of examples and counter-examples Asking for clarification	The classroom The lunch room The playground Standing in line Excursions

His research showed some evidence of internalisation and transfer of skills. There was a clear carry-over of the language used in philosophy into other subjects and settings. The increase was progressive. Phrases such as 'But you are just assuming that, you don't know for sure', and 'How do you know that?', and 'Why, what are your reasons?', had become part of his subjects' conversations. He concludes that:

> Since assumptions, presuppositions, asking for clarification and asking for reasons were activities pertaining to the philosophy program, it would be fair to say that the increase in the use of

these skills could be directly attributed to their exposure to philosophy. (Echeverria 1990)

Echeverria noted that when interviewing other teachers, they had mentioned that the students were more willing to ask questions, and the questions they asked were different, more original and creative.

An important point needs to be made about his findings. There is anecdotal evidence to suggest that the language skills learned via their involvement in philosophy are being applied by the children. However, whether the discussion of issues in class influences the children's other kinds of behaviors elsewhere is harder to determine.

> With regard to the internalization of the skills taught by the program, teachers agree that it is very difficult to measure, and that a way to promote it should be by taking up for discussion topics that affect children's lives directly and relating them to the philosophy class. Examples of these would be the issues that arise while they are standing in line, in the playground, lunch room, or at home. A teacher talked about the mob effect which occurs when children have internalized the behaviors that are appropriate under certain circumstances, but they do something else because it is more socially acceptable within their peer group. (Echeverria 1990)

Returning to the same issues repeatedly, which is what happens as students progress through the school doing philosophy, is one way of bringing about behavioral changes. There is a need for teachers to discuss the importance of consistency between behavior and stated beliefs, exploring inconsistencies of which they are aware.

Echeverria's research also pointed to teachers reporting that they were more comfortable taking risks like holding discussions for which they do not have all the answers and allowing children to ask questions that might be considered threatening in a traditional classroom.

6 TEACHERS' REFLECTIONS

A list of observations of teachers using the community of inquiry method was compiled at a Melbourne school. Some points made here can be used for reporting on individual children's involvement and skills, whilst others serve as a checklist for teachers' approaches. The teachers observed that the program had:

- provided a structure for good discussion
- provided time for thinking, questioning, listening and talking in large-group and small-group situations

- meant that teachers have changed the way they teach, in that they say less, listen harder and challenge more rigorously
- encouraged children to challenge each other's comments and thinking
- increased the contributions many children, even 'quiet ones', make in class, e.g. when compared with class chat time before starting the program
- helped increase confidence in some children, who otherwise are not confident contributors to class work
- changed the patterns of talk within the classroom to being much more student centred (the students talk more with each other rather than always speaking 'via' the teacher)
- demanded that children refine their language and word usage, and develop greater understanding of words and the meanings they attach to them
- developed maturity as children are given more responsibility for their own thinking, reasoning and discussion skills
- changed teaching elsewhere as teachers and children question, listen, and discuss better and search to have a better understanding of the vocabulary they use and its meaning
- shown children other ways of working and solving problems
- meant that the children enjoy the sessions, demand them in their week and do not respond to the bells to go to recess, preferring to remain in class
- stimulated children to continue their conversations in the playground

Another arena where the transference of skills of dialogue and thinking is being noticed is during conversations around the dinner table. Once the program begins, parents comment on changes they have noticed. The parents report instances in which their children had used skills that they didn't know they had. Skills such as pointing out contradictions, the exploration of a variety of points of view, and asking for reasons behind statements are some of the skills that parents are commenting on about their children's conversations at home.

Apart from changes noted in classrooms, teachers are reporting other changes, like the valuable team teaching sessions that result from the community of inquiry method. Another is the emerging need for a staff member to become a convenor of the school's philosophy program to help develop policy and coordinate programs and materials. A third major change has been the development of new curriculum policies which school councils have accepted.

CHAPTER FIVE

Units of Work

The following units of work have been designed to demonstrate the philosophical issues present in everyday literature. They have been devised to further the inquiry into a variety of issues raised by the stories or extracts and represent a variety of approaches used to foster inquiry. They are suitable for experienced classes or those just starting to use a community of inquiry. The year levels are suggestions only.

Famous Fables
Adapted and told by Honey Andersen

**A unit of work for years 4-6
by Gordon Money**

The Shepherd Boy and The Wolf (The Boy Who Cried Wolf)

Once there was a boy whose job was to watch over sheep as they grazed on the hillside. The boy liked jokes and sometimes he would run down to the village shouting, 'Help! There is a wolf attacking the sheep!' All the village people would run up the hillside to protect the sheep. But whenever they ran up the hill, they found there was no wolf there and the boy had only been joking.

One day, a wolf really did come and it started attacking the sheep. The boy ran quickly down the hill and shouted, 'Help! Help me! A wolf is attacking the sheep!' But the people all said, 'Oh it's only another joke,' and no-one would help him. The wolf destroyed all the sheep.

That day, the boy learned an important lesson. If you always tell lies, people will not believe you, even when you are telling the truth.

The aim of this first session is to get the children thinking about what truth means and what lies, tricks and jokes are. It encourages them to think about when teasing and joking go too far and who should be blamed for things that go wrong. They are also able to consider when it might be acceptable to lie to someone.

DISCUSSION

A liar is never believed, even when he/she is telling the truth.

* What is a lie?
* What is the truth?
* What is it to be honest? Is this different from being truthful?
* The shepherd boy thinks he is playing a joke on the village. When does a joke become a lie?
* When does joking or teasing go too far?
* A 'white lie' is one that is told to someone in order to prevent them from being hurt by the truth. Can it ever be all right to tell someone a lie?
* It is often seen as the parents' or guardians' fault when children misbehave or get into trouble. This is because parents are

considered responsible for their children. Who is responsible in this story? Is it the boy, or his parents and the other villagers who should have taken action earlier?

- How could the boy regain the trust of the villagers?

The North Wind and the Sun

The north wind and the sun had a competition to see who could be the first to persuade a traveller to take off his cloak. The north wind blew and blew. It tugged and flapped and tried to force the cloak from the man's shoulders. But the traveller just kept on hugging the cloak tighter and tighter to himself. He would not let his cloak go. Then the sun had a turn. As the sun shone, the rays warmed the traveller. He loosened the cloak as he walked, then finally he sat down and took it off.

'There,' said the sun. 'Gentle persuasion always works better than force!'

DISCUSSION

Gentle persuasion is always better than force.

- What are some examples where this would be true?
- What are some examples where force may be better than gentle persuasion?
- Sometimes in wars attempts are made to come to agreement through gentle persuasion in the form of peace talks. How is the story similar to a war situation?
- Is it dishonest to persuade someone to do something they may not want to do, without them realising what you are doing?

STUDENT ACTIVITIES

1 Try to gently persuade a partner to do or say something they do not want to do. In doing so, explain to them the reasons why you think they should do it and listen to their reasons why they don't want to do it. Was it easy to refrain from using forceful language and actions?

2 Try to gently persuade a partner to do or say something without them realising what you are trying to get them to do or say. Then see how easy it is to get them to do or say something by using force of some sort. (Not rough!)

These two activities are designed to illustrate how, with most situations, it is more productive to use gentle, passive persuasion rather than force.

The Fox and The Crow

One day, a fox noticed a crow sitting in a tree, holding a large lump of cheese in its beak. The fox was hungry and he decided he would try to get the cheese from the crow.

'Hello!' he called, looking up at the crow. 'How beautiful you are! Your lovely wing feathers are gleaming in the sunlight, and your eyes are so bright. You look so strong and graceful sitting there! I wonder if a bird as beautiful as you can sing well too?'

The crow was so pleased to hear this flattery that she immediately opened her beak to sing for him. The cheese fell out and the cunning fox snatched it up and ate it at once.

The crow flew sadly away. 'I've learned a lesson from that,' she thought. 'I'll never be taken in by flattery again.'

DISCUSSION

The following questions are designed to raise the issues of flattery, honest opinions, truth, and the advantages and disadvantages of flattery.

- The crow learned never to be taken in by flattery. What is flattery? How is it different from praise?
- Is flattery still the truth (what the person really thinks) or is it more than this?
- What are the advantages and disadvantages of giving, and of receiving flattery?
- Flattery is praising someone too much. Praise can be merited, but if we praise people more than they deserve, we are said to flatter them. Which of the following sentences are praise, flattery, or something else?

1 Your house is the grandest in the neighborhood.
2 The person who created the Frisbee was brilliant.
3 The neighbor who risked her life to save a child from a burning house is a hero.
4 You have a terrific voice, you should be in the choir.
5 You were so clever to get all your spelling right, no-one else could do that.

The Mice in Council

There were once some mice who lived in a house where there was a large cat. They were frightened of the cat and called a meeting to try to decide what to do about it. There were many suggestions but the best idea came from one of the youngest mice. 'Why not hang a bell around his neck?' the mouse suggested. 'That way, we'll hear him when he walks around.'

All the mice thought it was a great idea. They patted the young mouse on the back and told him he was clever. They all wished they'd thought of the idea themselves. Then an old mouse stood up. 'There's just one problem,' he said. 'Who is going to hang the bell around the cat's neck?'

DISCUSSION

Through the following discussion, students can examine what taking a risk means and why people do so. There are also other philosophical issues such as the decision-making process and how decision makers often put others at risk.

- Tying a bell around the cat's neck would be a risk for the mice. There are many different sorts of risks people take. What are some of them? (safety risks, financial risks, etc.)
- When people take risks, others usually think of them as either courageous or foolish. What is the difference between a courageous and a foolish risk?
- What are some characteristics of a good solution, a good decision and a good idea?

A SOLUTION TO A PROBLEM

Can you think of a time when you came up with a good solution to a problem but found that your solution presented another problem Discuss this in a small group. Try to think up alternative solutions to the problem which would not cause added problems.

The Ass's Shadow

One very hot day in the desert, a young man hired an ass to carry him to the next town. It was a long way and the journey was hot and uncomfortable. About midday, it was so hot that the young man dismounted and tried to lie down in the ass's shadow. However, the owner who was leading the ass stopped the young man. 'You can't sit there,' he said. 'The shadow belongs to me. You hired the ass, not the shadow.'

'But I hired the ass for the journey,' replied the young man. 'Surely the shadow is mine as well.'

The men argued and argued. They didn't notice the ass as it ran away.

In this session students could be asked to contribute their personal relevant anecdotes and assess the story for its believability. Personal rights and general human rights could also be examined. The activity below provides good practice at healthy debating and encourages the students to learn to negotiate disputes and think of solutions to problems such as the one in the story.

DISCUSSION

- Is this a good story? Why? Why not?
- Does it seem believable?
- Does arguing in this way solve problems?
- In the story, how good is the argument the ass's driver puts forward: 'You didn't hire the ass's shadow.'
- Is there a better way to sort out disputes like the one in the story?
- What is a right?
- What are some things you see as your personal rights?
- Are there any rights you believe you have that you don't believe others should have?
- What are rights you think all people should have?
- What are some rights that you feel particular people should not have?

ACTIVITY

In pairs, assume the roles of the ass's driver and the man who hired it, and attempt to resolve the dispute without an endless argument, but with a sensible progressive discussion. Report any solutions you have come up with to the class, and explain how you came to that agreement.

The Lion and the Mouse

One hot, sunny day a lion was dozing in the sun. He felt a small animal run across his face.

'Stop tickling,' he grumbled and he grabbed at the creature. He saw it was a tiny mouse, and he opened his mouth lazily to eat her.

'Stop!' she cried. 'Don't eat me! I'm so small, I'm no meal for a creature as large as you. If you free me, someday I promise I will reward you.'

'Whatever could a mouse do for a lion?' he asked. 'But I will let you go, as you are right about one thing! You are not much of a meal for a lion!' And he opened his paws and let her escape.

Sometime later, the mouse was foraging in the jungle when she heard a lion roaring. She ran to see what was the matter, and to her amazement, found the very same lion caught in a net. 'Don't worry,' she called, 'I can help you escape.'

'How can someone as small as you help?' the lion asked despairingly.

'I'll show you,' she said. And she began gnawing at the ropes. Soon the ropes were bitten through and the lion was free. 'Thank you,' he said.

'You were once kind to me,' said the mouse, 'and I have always remembered your kindness.'

DISCUSSION

Through engaging in the activities and exercises below students should be able to discuss issues such as promises, kindness, gratitude and expectations of themselves and others in relation to these issues.

- The mouse makes a promise to the lion that may have been difficult to keep. Should you make promises if you are not sure you can keep them?
- Is it ever all right to not keep a promise? Under what circumstances?
- The mouse shows gratitude towards the lion. What is the difference between gratitude and kindness?

The Dog and the Meat

One day, a large dog stole a bone from a butcher. As he scurried away, he had to cross a bridge over a river. He looked over the edge of the bridge into the river and saw his reflection. He thought it was another dog with a bone. 'I'll steal that bone too,' he thought.

He opened his mouth to steal the other bone, but his bone dropped into the river. Afterwards he thought about what had happened. 'If I hadn't been so greedy, I would have at least had one bone,' he decided. 'Greediness gets you nowhere.'

DISCUSSION

The main issue within this story is greed. Questions encourage discussion about the advantages and disadvantages of being greedy, and the differences in being greedy in relation to animals and humans. Another issue is thinking about the consequences of our actions. There is also the opportunity to discuss what is real and what is an illusion.

The story concludes that 'greediness gets you nowhere'.

- What is greed?
- Do you believe that greed gets you nowhere?
- Can greed ever be considered a good thing? Under what circumstances?
- In the text a dog is being greedy. Is greed different for animals and humans?
- The second piece of meat the dog saw was not real, although he thought it was. When is something real? When is it an illusion? How do we know if something is one or the other?

The Bald Rider

There was once a man who was so ashamed about being bald, that he bought a wig. He wore the wig all the time and never once let anyone see his bald head. One day he was out riding his horse with a group of friends when a gust of wind blew his wig right off. Everyone laughed when they saw he was completely bald, but so did the man.

'How silly,' he said. 'How could I expect anyone else's hair to stay on my head when my own hair fell off?' From that day, he never wore a wig again. 'I must learn to accept myself just as I am,' he told the others.

Invite the students to look at the fable and decide whether they agree with the message it gives and what exceptions there may be to this. It looks at the issues of vanity, appearance and reality.

DISCUSSION

- The story tells us that we should always be satisfied with what we have. Do you agree with this?
- Do you think that the man should have been satisfied with what he had?
- Vanity is excessive pride. Do you think the rider was vain?
- Why do many people not like others to know they are wearing a wig or have had a hair transplant?
- Would you consider it vain for a child who has lost their hair through chemotherapy treatment for cancer to wear a wig?
- Should we try to give a false impression about what we really are like? Is it dishonest to do so?
- Is it all right for people to change their appearance if they are not happy with it?

APPEARANCE AND REALITY

1 Can you think of something that isn't really the way it looks?
2 Could other people see the same thing differently from you?
3 Would you know if something did not look the way it really is?
5 Does it matter to you that some things look different from the way they really are?

Tuck Everlasting
by Natalie Babbitt

A unit of work for years 5-7
by Fred Carstens

The following is a summary of the story *Tuck Everlasting*

Winnie Foster is an only child living in a cottage at the edge of a wood in a small country town. She is over protected by her parents, and is not allowed out of the garden. She spends a lot of time watching from her side of the fence. Her only companion is a toad which she observes and talks to. She tells him she plans to run away.

One evening, while she is talking to a stranger who is loitering near the wood, they both hear strange music which her grandmother insists is the music of elves. Next morning, after overcoming her doubts, she ventures into the wood. She sees the toad and then stumbles upon a young, handsome man whom she watches drinking from a hidden spring.

Winnie reveals herself and attempts to drink from the spring, but the young man will not let her drink. An old woman and another boy suddenly appear and they pull Winnie onto their horse and ride away with her. Sometime later they stop and explain that the spring had enchanted water. Anything who drinks from it will live forever. They are the Tuck family, and eighty-seven years ago they drank from the spring. Now neither can age nor die.

The Tucks insist on taking Winnie to the cottage where Angus and Mae Tuck, the parents, live so that they can explain how important it is for Winnie never to tell anyone of the existence of the spring. Mae shows Winnie her music box and Winnie realises the elven music is really music from this music box. Neither the Tucks nor Winnie realise that the stranger from the previous evening had been following Winnie and had overheard the whole story. He follows them to the Tucks' cottage.

The Tucks set about explaining the horror of being immortal to Winnie. She is reassured and grows confident of their goodness and of the fact they will return her to her home. The stranger meanwhile has returned to Winnie's home and has arranged to be given the Wood, which contains the enchanted spring, in exchange for showing the police where Winnie has been taken. The stranger hopes to make his fortune selling water from the spring of eternal life.

The stranger arrives at the Tucks' cottage and tries to remove Winnie. He explains how he now owns the Wood and he plans to sell the spring water.

Winnie refuses to go with him, and Mae Tuck, in defending Winnie, knocks the stranger unconscious just as the policeman arrives. Mae is taken to prison and Winnie is returned to her parents. The stranger dies and Mae is to be hanged.

Winnie helps to rescue Mae whose sons pull out the prison window and help her to escape. Winnie spends a night in the bed in the prison cell to enable the Tucks to have time to escape. The plan succeeds.

Jesse Tuck has given Winnie a small bottle of spring water to keep until she is seventeen so that she can drink it and become his wife, but instead Winnie uses it to save her friend, the toad, who has been mortally injured by a dog.

Many years later Mr and Mrs Tuck pass through the town once more. They visit the graveyard and notice Winnie's grave. She had died at the age of 78.

This novel is packed with philosophical issues. What follows are examples of issues in chapters 1, 2 and 3 and suggested follow-up activities.

■ WHAT CAN THINK?

The road swung out in a wide arc as if ... it had reason to think where it was going.

- We know humans can think, but what about other living things and objects? Is it possible, for instance, that a road could think?
- Which of the following ways of thinking — ideas, predictions, ramblings, conclusions — do you think might apply to inanimate objects?
- What does 'to think' mean? Do you ever think about your own thinking? How could you explain to someone else what thinking means? How would you explain to someone else what thinking means?
- Do animals think? Is it the same way humans think? How would you support your view about this? What about inanimate objects such as a robot or a computer? Do they think?
- What distinguishes humans from animals and computers? Classify the listed words describing thinking into:

words	done by humans	done by animals	done by computers	done by all three
hope worry contemplate wonder reason decide dream imagine remember conclude				

Can you think of situations in which these kinds of thinking occur?

■ *BELONGING/PROPERTY/OWNERSHIP*

... the road no longer belonged to the cows...
... the wood belonged to the Foster s...
... ownership of land is an odd thing
... How deep after all can it go?

- When we own land, how much do we own? Can you do whatever you like with it? Is it the same as your bike belonging to you?
- Use one of the following categories to say to what extent we own the listed things. Be sure to give your reasons. (Adapted from Lipman 1980)

	completely	partly	not at all
a book a cat a dream our hair (before cutting) our hair (after cutting) a tree another person things we say			

- Do our parents own us?
- How can you tell the difference between something your family owns and something you own?
- Is there a difference between things people own, and things no-one owns?

Q. Do I belong to my body or does my body belong to me?

My thoughts: I don't think that my body belongs to me or that I belong to my body. I don't think that anyone owns anyone's body because our body is part of us. I don't think you can own something that is part of you. You cannot own your finger because it is part of you. It is you. If part of you was cut off then you would own it. If part of a piece of paper was chopped off the rest of the paper would own it. It is your finger because it is no longer part of you. The same with the paper.

■ DREAMS

Tuck reluctantly awakes from a dream in which the family were in heaven and had never heard of Treegap.

- What is a dream?
- What is the difference between a dream you have when asleep and a day-dream?
- Tuck says: 'Anyways I can't help what I dream.' Is this true?
- Mac says, 'It's no use having that dream ... nothings going to change.' Are dreams of any use?

With which of the following statements do you agree?

- Things you dream about have happened in your life.
- Dreams can foretell the future. Some people never dream.
- Dreams can make you feel happy or sad.
- Dreams are usually about things you could never do.

■ REASONS

It is often important to be able to give reasons for our opinions if we want others to consider them. We also need to believe that the opinions we have are worth having. We need to give reasons to help other people understand why we hold the views we do. Sometimes several good reasons are needed.

- Mae Tuck intends to ride to meet the boys even though she agrees with Tuck that she had 'better not do that'. Look at the reasons she gives for going. [Quote from text] Are they acceptable reasons? Are they sufficient in this instance?

- Are there times you do things when you know there are reasons you shouldn't? Why?
- What makes a reason a good reason?

REMEMBER

Mae Tuck says '... even if someone did see me, they won't remember. They never did before ...'

- What is the difference between a verbs like *baking* and *throwing* and the verbs *remembering* and *thinking*?
- Why is it that no-one has ever remembered Mae?
- Is remembering the same as having memories?

RESENTMENT

Sometimes we might be angry with ourselves, but take it out on someone else. People sometimes do not want to accept responsibility for their actions and blame someone else. The toad is given the attribute of feeling resentful.

- How do you know when someone feels resentment?
- What evidence is there in the story that the toad is resentful?
- If there is no outward evidence of resentment, how do you know it is felt?
- Can animals or other things feel resentful?
- From the feelings listed, choose the most appropriate term in the following instances: anger, resentment, responsible, sorrow
  Your pet dog dies.
  Your best friend teases you.
  You are wrongly accused of stealing a bag.
  After many attempts to ride a surfboard you are told to give up.
  Your voice cracks whilst singing solo at the school concert.
- If you had an awful haircut would you resent it if the other kids in the class teased you? What would you do about it?
- Are there times when it's okay to feel resentful?

NAMES

'It would be nice to have a new name... one that's not at all worn out from being used so much.'

- If you didn't have a name, would it matter to you?
- If you had a different name, would you be a different person?

- If people wanted to, could they rename everything in the world?
- Do people look like their name?

WHO DO YOU THINK YOU ARE?

- Are you:
  what you do?
  all the things you have done in your life?
  your personality?
  your thoughts?
  something else?
- Would you be the same person you are now if you had different parents?
- If you cut your nails, or lose a tooth, do you lose part of yourself?
- When you think of a new idea, do you gain a new part of yourself?
- Are you really the person your parents, your teachers, your friends think you are?

DECISIONS

Winnie says, 'And I might even decide to have a pet.' In this example Winnie chooses to decide.

- How do you decide what you will or won't do?
- Can you imagine a world in which no decisions are made?
- Think of an example of a time you made a wrong decision. What made it wrong?

The Haunting
by Margaret Mahy

A unit of work for years 5-7
by Maurice Ryan

Following is a summary of *The Haunting.*

Barney is an eight-year-old boy whose mother died as he was born. He is now living with his two sisters, Troy and Tabitha, and his father and step-mother Claire, who is pregnant. Barney is a quiet, gentle boy who is very attached to Claire. He secretly worries that she too may die having her baby.

One day Barney hears and sees a ghostly figure, a voice which tells him 'Barnaby's dead. I'm going to be very lonely.' Barney is disturbed by this apparition. He thinks it is telling him he is about to die, as his real name is Barnaby. When he reaches home he learns his Great-Uncle Barnaby has died. Barney faints and causes quite a stir amongst the members of his family.

Barney has three sets of Grandparents, but it is the Scholars, the grandparents of his dead mother, and Great Grandma Scholar, whom the children don't particularly like. Great-Uncle Barnaby was a Scholar and the children knew he had two other brothers as well. However Troy, the quiet, organised sister, produces a family photograph which shows there was another brother as well. He bears an uncanny resemblance to Barney. Tabitha, the outspoken and curious sister, is entranced by the thought of a missing great uncle.

The family visit the Scholar house to offer condolences for Great-Uncle Barnaby's death, and Tabitha asks about the missing great-uncle. She is told his name was Cole and he had been dead for a long time. Barney becomes aware during the visit that he is being watched by all the Scholar relations and this makes him very uncomfortable. He is given a book to look at and writing appears which only he and Tabitha see.

Barney later talks to Tabitha about the voices and for a while feels better, but the voices and visions keep returning, and the voice begins to tell Barney it is coming for him. Over the next week Barney becomes more and more frightened. Footsteps come closer and closer and even Tabitha can hear them when she is with Barney. Tabitha urges Barney to tell Claire, who is worried about Barney's strange behavior, but Barney refuses as he does not want to worry her. Tabitha confides in Great-Uncle Guy who explains that the Scholar family has always had magicians, and that Great-Uncle Cole was one of them. Great-Uncle Guy thinks Barney may be becoming the next family magician. He also tells her Great-Uncle Cole is not dead at all, and that he had been in contact with Great-Uncle Barnaby.

Eventually the story comes out, and Barney is able to share his fears with the family. He tells his father that Cole wants to take him away and his father reassures him that he would never allow Barney to be taken.

Cole appears at the house and frightens the family. He performs a trick to prove to Claire that he is a magician. Miraculously, the whole Scholar family appear and arguments break out. Barney is so afraid that Cole might hurt someone, he offers to go with Cole. Just at that moment, Troy stuns everyone with the evidence that it is she who has magic powers. She tells of events that happened long ago and explains how she'd promised her mother before she died that she would never let on she had the magic powers. Troy explains how Great Grandma Scholar is also a magician but after a terrible accident she'd set out to crush the magic out of herself. She couldn't bear to see it in others. Troy and Great-Uncle Cole become friends and Barney is left to be the gentle, sensitive boy he always was.

SESSION ONE: IMAGINARY AND REAL

When, suddenly, on an ordinary Wednesday, it seemed to Barney that the world tilted and ran downhill in all directions, he knew he was about to be haunted again. It had happened when he was younger but he had thought that being haunted was a babyish thing that you grew out of, like crying when you fell over, or not having a bike. 'Remember Barney's imaginary friends, Mantis, Bigbuzz and Ghost?' Clair — his stepmother — sometimes said. 'The garden seems empty now that they've gone. I quite miss them.'

But she was really pleased perhaps because, being so very real to Barney, they had become too real for her to laugh over. Barney had been sorry to lose them, but he wanted Claire to feel comfortable living with him. He could not remember his own mother and Claire had come as a wonderful surprise, giving him a hug when he came home from school, asking him about his day, telling him about hers, arranging picnics and unexpected parties and helping him with hard homework. It seemed worth losing Mantis, Bigbuzz and Ghost and the other kind phantoms that had been his friends for so many days before Claire came.

Activities
- Is an imaginary friend still a friend?
- What is so special about a secret friend?
- Does unreal mean the same thing as imaginary?

- Are reflections real?
- Draw a picture of your best friend. Is that really your best friend?

SESSION TWO: FAMILY RESEMBLANCES AND RELATIONSHIP

'All this is by the way,' Claire said, 'because you're going to have to come home anyway, Tabitha. We're going to visit your Scholar grandparents this afternoon, just to pay our respects as they've lost Great-Uncle Barnaby.'

'Oh no! Do we have to?' Tabitha screwed up her face as if in agony. 'They're nice and all that! I do like them, but they're so sort of papery, if you know what I mean.'

'How you do go on, Tabitha!' Claire replied. 'It's very wearing. Look — they're your grandparents, and Great-Uncle Barnaby was your great-uncle, your grandfather's brother.'

'Not good enough!' declared Tabitha. 'Not enough reason to make us waste a Saturday afternoon just being polite.'

'They like seeing us,' said Troy.

'They must be mad!' exclaimed Tabitha. 'None of us is beautiful. You're bony, I'm fat and Barney is like one of those ordinary brown dogs you see everywhere, nothing special. Of course you remember them more than I do so it's probably not such a waste of time for you.' Tabitha marmaladed her toast in a fretful way. 'Suppose just Claire and Dad and you and Barney go and I stay at the swimming pool improving my diving? That's four-fifths polite. Plenty!'

'Tabitha — stop it! You know you have to go,' Claire said. 'No arguments! I rang last night and said we'd all go and see them. I don't want them to think I'm trying to keep you all to myself. You still belong to them too, you know.'

'But it's just a sort of accident,' whined Tabitha. 'Families are accidental. I mean — look at me, look at Troy! Dead opposites really, and ...'

'Tabitha,' Claire cried, 'I'm going to be steady and stern with you. We are all — I repeat all — going to visit the Scholars this afternoon. And now let's change the subject. Barney — you're very quiet this morning.'

'There's no space to say anything when Tabitha's around,' Barney replied. 'If I say something — well I'm always talking at the same time as she is.'

'It's not as if you ever have anything interesting to say,' Tabitha replied at once. 'I mean, you're old enough to speak but too young to have any brains. You've only been interesting five times in your life — no, six counting yesterday and —' Troy bumped Tabitha on the head with her knuckles.

Activities

The issue of family resemblances might easily lead on to 'nature vs nurture'. In addition, there is the issue of our relations with our family. These issues are very relevant to students. Take care that the discussion doesn't tend to be exclusive of non-nuclear families. In this respect, the blended family in the text is a good role model.

- Are Tabitha's reasons for not wishing to visit her grandparents justified?
- Can you have nothing in common with your brother or sister?
- If you look like your brother or sister, does that make you closer?
- Should we be loyal to our family no matter what?
- How far does family extend?

SESSION THREE: TALKING AND WORDS — DO WE TALK TOO MUCH/TOO LITTLE?

'Perhaps he drowned himself,' Tabitha suggested, trying as usual to make life dramatic and alarming.

'Perhaps he did,' agreed Great-Uncle Guy, surprisingly. 'We'll never know. He certainly wasn't a very happy boy — though I don't want to go into just why he wasn't happy, if you don't mind, Tabitha.'

'Yes, Tabitha — that's quite enough,' said Claire. 'You do — you really do — talk far too much.'

Tabitha grinned at her grandmother.

'I know I do,' she answered. 'Everyone's always telling me I do and really and truly, I don't mean to. Today I meant to hide away and be silent like Troy. But there are so many questions and words, someone's got to use them or they might go rusty or get mould on them or something.'

'Claire, I like to hear her talk,' said Grandma Scholar, 'and I don't get much chance. Come with me Tabby and help with the afternoon tea and tell me about your notebook at the same time.'

Activities

The issue of talking was raised by Barney and is further developed by Tabitha here. This discussion has a lot of potential for exploring the issue of talking and how it relates to thinking. Children will reflect on something that they may not have considered greatly before. In addition the issue of words, their nature and their uses should interest everyone.

- Do we have to have quiet people and talkative people like Barney and Tabitha?
- Could words get 'rusty and mouldy' if nobody used them?

- Do we think in words like we talk in words?
- Could we do with more words or fewer words?
- Are there some things that there are no words for?
- Could you have a friend with whom you didn't talk?

SESSION FOUR: CONTROLLING WHAT WE THINK

After Claire had come in and read him a story, kissed him good night and turned the light out, he lay in the darkness trying not to think either backwards or forwards. Instead he closed his eyes and tried to make sleep come quickly. It wasn't his usual drowsy drifting but a watchful sentry-duty sort of waiting. A dream might come and refuse to give the password. Then he could drive it away. The darkness behind his eyelids was streaked with lights like dim, slow fireworks going off, and it was impossible to feel sleepy. A face flashed into his mind and was gone again, but he knew the face well. It was the face in a photograph of his mother, Dove, which stood on the dressing table in Troy's room. Barney wondered if it was Dove who was haunting him, perhaps angry because he had grown so fond of Claire. However he could not really believe she would mind. She looked too cheerful for that. And anyway, because of the message, he was certain that he was being haunted because Great-Uncle Barnaby had died. Something was being required of him, but he could not think what it might be.

'It's no use bothering about it,' he told himself sternly and saw his own words float by, lighting up his shut-eyed darkness with letters of fire.

'Think different!' he commanded his anxious mind. 'Different!' he said aloud, to hear his own determination. It was very convincing and he opened his eyes to clear his head by staring into the real outside darkness. The rockets and fiery letters vanished.

'A circus!' he commanded, and shut his eyes again. No circus came into his head, but something nearly as good, for he found himself remembering a Punch and Judy show he had once seen.

Pink and white curtains flew open and Punch squeaked and waved a stick. Barney made himself remember Judy, the baby, a crocodile and a policeman. His memories began to run out and he was still not asleep. But somehow he could not stop watching the Punch and Judy show. The tiny curtains swept closed and then opened again on another scene — not on a puppet play but on a real place, one that Barney had never seen before. This was not something from his own mind, but something that someone was deliberately showing him. Barney was being haunted again.

Activities

Barney's struggle with his thoughts raises the issue of thinking. In Barney's case he tried to 'think different' but he is being haunted and can't help what he thinks. The discussion would hopefully lead to control of our thoughts.

- Can we control our thoughts?
- Can somebody else control our thoughts? How do you know?
- Do we control our thoughts or our thoughts control us?
- How could Barney know something was being required of him yet not know what it was?
- Are there some things you can't stop thinking about?
- Are there some things you would like to think about but can't?

Using fairytales to examine 'good' and 'bad'

A unit of work for Prep year
by Elizabeth Edmonds

Objectives

- To involve the children in identifying good and bad characters in fairytales.
- To develop an understanding of good and bad actions
- To examine the actions, beliefs and values that make a character good or bad.
- The children will be able to name three characters they think are bad and three they think are good and justify their choices.

Key questions

- What makes us feel good?
- What makes us feel bad?
- What is a good character?
- What is a bad character?
- What makes a character
- What makes a character good?
- What actions do characters perform that are good?
- What actions do characters perform that are bad?
- What causes good and bad actions?

SESSION ONE: THE THREE PIGS

Activities

The terms *good* and *bad* have many different meanings in our society. Sometimes these differences are not clear. Try some of these ideas and see how the children understand the difference between good and bad.

1 Read a favorite version of the story.

Whole class sharing and inquiry: Ask the children:

'Was it good for the wolf to blow down the pigs' houses?'

'What can you tell me about the sort of character the wolf was?'

The children discuss the questions. After each child has made a comment or asked a question, another member of their circle is chosen to comment or question the ideas expressed. For example:

Child A: 'I think the wolf was mean because he scared the pigs.'

He then chooses Child B who might say:

David Stanley

① Donald Duck does something wrong wrong

One day Donald was smoking witch was wrong.

② Donald Duck does someting bad. One day Donald did grfete on a wall and that was bad.

'Yes, I know what you mean. He was sneaky when he went up the chimney.'

2 Game: 'Who am I?' (to develop questioning skills)

You need four simple masks or puppets of the characters.

Take the puppet of the wolf and face it away from the children. The children ask questions to try to identify the puppet and you are only allowed to answer yes or no. For example:

Teacher: *Who am I ?*
Children: *Am I mean?*
                  Am I clever?

Repeat the game for each character. In this way the children are establishing a character description

3 Cooperative group work: In groups, the children discuss how the pigs would have been feeling when the wolf was blowing down the houses. Why would the pigs would have felt that way?

The children draw the pigs in the house. The children draw the pigs' facial expressions to reflect their thinking/feeling.

4 Whole class sharing and inquiry: The children come back to the class circle. The reporters report on the group discussion. The children come to conclusions on the ending of the story, although they may achieve consensus. This is discussed in the whole share group.

SESSION TWO: JACK AND THE BEANSTALK

1 Read a favorite version of the story.
Have the children take it in turns to act out the story with puppets as you retell the story.

2 Game: 'Jeopardy'
Draw characters and objects from the story on the blackboard.

hen	giant	harp
Jack	beanstalk	Jack's mum
giant's wife	golden harp	man who sold the cow

Divide the class into two teams: naughts and crosses.
Each team has a turn alternately to identify/describe the pictures. The children choose a character/object from the pictures and have to tell the grade everything they know about the character/object.
When a child accurately identifies/describes the character/object the teacher puts a cross through the pictures or a circle on the picture.
The first team to have three of their symbols in a row wins.

3 Whole class sharing and inquiry circle: Begin the discussion by focusing on WHY questions. Use the Jack puppet to discuss Jack using why questions. The children ask WHY questions about the text which are recorded on the board. The children vote on which question they would like to discuss. For example:
Why did Jack climb the beanstalk?
Why did Jack take those things from the giant?
Each child takes it in turns to speak. After each child has made a comment or asked a question they choose another member of the group to do the same.

4 Class graph: In the share circle the children decide upon a color to represent GOOD and a color to represent BAD. They do this by suggesting and explaining which color they think represents good or bad. Provide each child with a picture of Jack. If they think he was good, color him _____. If they think he was bad, color him _____.
The children put their pictures onto a class picture graph.

5 Sharing and inquiry circle: The children discuss the graph asking each other to justify their choice of what Jack was ... GOOD or BAD.
The graph could be extended to include the giant. Using the

colors the children decided on they could color in pictures of the giant. Add these pictures to the graph.

CONSOLIDATION AND EVALUATION ACTIVITIES

1 The children vote on a character they wish to discuss from any fairytale. (They may have time to discuss several characters).

They use Edward De Bono's six hats to discuss the characters.

When responding to a discussion point the children choose which hat they are going to wear. When wearing a particular hat they focus on those issues. For example, when they are wearing the yellow hat they discuss the character's positive actions.

When they are wearing the black hat they look at the negative actions of the character.

When they are wearing the red hat they talk about how they feel about the character and his/her actions.

The children complete a worksheet where they have to categorise characters according to their own criteria.

2 The children create a fairytale house. They have to consider which characters are the good characters and which characters are the bad characters. They also have to consider how one character might affect another character. They have to decide which characters should and which shouldn't go together. In the share circle the children consider the above issues.

The Cabbage Patch Fib
by Paul Jennings

**A unit of work for years 1 and 2
by Tracey Jolly**

The following is a summary of *The Cabbage Patch Fib*.

> One night at the dinner table, eight-year-old Chris asked his father, 'Where do babies come from?' His father told him that babies grow in cabbage patches and Chris believed him. That night, in the cabbage patch, Chris found a baby. The baby was bright green and it thought Chris was his father. If anyone else held the baby, it stopped breathing, so that Chris had to take care of it. He stayed away from school and became quite famous.
>
> After a couple of weeks, the novelty of looking after the baby wore off and Chris wanted to able to do all the things he usually did. He decided to put the baby back in the cabbage patch. He left the baby but it held its breath and nearly died. Only when Chris returned did it begin to breathe again. Chris and his sister sat for hours in the cabbage patch trying to think of a solution to Chris's problem. Just as all seemed hopeless, they noticed that one of the cabbages had grown to an enormous size. A door opened in the cabbage and a small green woman rushed out and grabbed the baby. Chris was pleased that the baby had found its own people.
>
> A few nights later, his sister heard Chris up in the night again. He was on the roof looking for the storks that deliver babies. Dad had told him that this is REALLY where babies come from. His sister told him the truth and he believed her. The story ends with Chris going off to enlighten his dad.

SESSION ONE: DISTINCTIONS

> I once read of a duck that thought it was a rabbit because the first thing it saw after it hatched out was a rabbit. This is the same thing.

- Is it possible for a duck to think it's a rabbit?
- In what ways are the duck and rabbit different?
- Does that mean they have nothing in common?
- What are the differences between a cat and a dog?
- What are the differences between two cats?
- What do you think is the best way to describe the differences between a cats and dogs?

SESSION TWO: PRIVATE FEELINGS

> Mum looked sad. ' I don't know what we can do, Chris. It won't let anyone touch it except you. You don't want it to die, do you?' Chris didn't answer. He picked up the baby and stomped off.

Children (and adults) frequently jump to conclusions about how a person is feeling, based on their actions. Sometimes these conclusions are based on a sound analysis, other times they are quick, irrational statements. This discussion should help children think about the conclusions they draw, and hopefully get them to think about another's feelings, before they make any rash statements.

- Does anyone know your feelings better than you do?
- How do you know that others think and feel?
- Would you like to know what another child thinks and feels?
- Should an author tell you the private feelings of a character in their story?

> I think the story is trying to say, if you tease somebody it will always come back to you and make you regret it. And it also says that before you say something to somebody, think to yourself, is it offending him if I say it, or will it imbarase him infront of everybody. It also says that you are pretty stupid to say bad things to people who are younger than you and might take it worse than you thought.

SESSION THREE: TRUTH AND LIES

> 'Well,' said Mum. 'Do you know the truth about babies now?'
> 'I'm going to have a little talk with poor old Dad,' he said. 'It's about time somebody told him the truth.'

This is a topic which will promote a lot of discussion, as lies are something which should be familiar to all children! Lies are not only told by children; adults also tell them. Sometimes a person may lie based on good intentions, and in instances such as this, is it still a bad thing to tell a lie? Reasons for lying should also be taken into account.

- What is a lie?
- Is it ever okay to lie?
- Is there a difference between a lie and a fib?
- When Dad told Chris that babies grow under cabbages and that storks drop them down chimneys, was that a lie, a fib, or something else?
- Why do you think Dad told Chris that?
- What is the 'truth'?
- Can the truth be something different to different people?

Alice's Adventures in Wonderland
by Lewis Carroll

A unit of work for years 4 - 8
by Manuel Augustin

The story of Alice, the little girl who dreams that she pursues the White Rabbit down a rabbit hole and meets with strange adventures and odd characters provides a huge range of material suitable for philosophical discussion. The following activities are based on Chapter 5: Advice from a Caterpillar, and Chapter 7: A Mad Tea-Party. These two chapters contain wonderful and stimulating areas for children to discuss, such as personal identity, social norms, the concept of time, contradictions, and many others.

SESSION ONE: PERSONAL IDENTITY

> The Caterpillar and Alice looked at each other for some time in silence: at last the Caterpillar took the hookah out of its mouth, and addressed her in a languid, sleepy voice.
>
> 'Who *are* you?' said the Caterpillar.
>
> This was not an encouraging opening for a conversation. Alice replied, rather shyly, 'I — I hardly know, Sir, just at present — at least I know who I *was* when I got up this morning, but I think I must have been changed several times since then.'
>
> 'What do you mean by that?' said the Caterpillar, sternly. 'Explain yourself!'
>
> 'I can't explain *myself*, I'm afraid, Sir,' said Alice, 'because I'm not myself, you see.'

1 Ask the class: 'What makes you, you?' Write suggestions on the board, and then have children vote for the five most popular ideas to be put on a shortlist.

2 Children form five groups to discuss one of the five ideas . Give them time to find reasons whether their idea of what constitutes someone's personal identity is a valid one. Some suggested focus points might be:
   one's name
   personality
   physical looks

brain
memories and personal beliefs
soul

3 The groups then bring their reasons and justifications to the class. Students conduct the discussions using the guidelines for community of inquiry, and questioning, querying, challenging and putting forward opposing views.

SESSION TWO: CHANGE

'I'm afraid I can't put it more clearly,' Alice replied, very politely, 'for I can't understand it myself, to begin with; and being so many different sizes in a day is very confusing.'
'It isn't,' said the Caterpillar.
'Well, perhaps you haven't found it so yet,' said Alice; 'but when you have to turn into a chrysalis — you will be some day you know — and then after that a butterfly, I should think you'll feel it a little queer, won't you?'

- Students could work in groups to decide if there has been a change and if so, what type of change? (i.e. what form does this change take).
  a seed becoming a tree
  winter becoming spring
  ice becoming liquid water
  a girl becoming a woman or a boy becoming a man

SESSION THREE: DIFFERENCES AND SIMILARITIES

Does change make things different? Students could work in groups to discuss this ideas, and to classify the following into one of three categories provided.

	Very different	Somewhat different	No difference
1. A caterpillar and the butterfly	....	....	....
2. A tadpole and the frog	....	....	....
3. You and your brother/sister	....	....	....
4. You and your neighbor	....	....	....
5. You and your shadow	....	....	....
6. You today and you 5 years ago	....	....	....
7. You today and last week	....	....	....
8. You today and in 10 years	....	....	....

Discussion points:

- Is a caterpillar the same as the butterfly it changes into? Is it the same creature?
- If not, what happened to the caterpillar?
- If so, why do we call it a butterfly rather than a caterpillar?

You could list differences and similarities between a caterpillar and butterfly on the board.

SESSION FOUR: RELATIVITY

'Well, I should like to be a *little* larger, Sir, if you wouldn't mind,' said Alice: 'three inches is such a wretched height to be.'

'It is a very good height indeed!' said the Caterpillar angrily, rearing itself upright as it spoke (it was exactly three inches high).

- Pose these two questions and let students explore the idea of how things are described relative to each other.

    Why does Alice think three inches is a wretched height to be?

    Why does the caterpillar think it is a very good height?

How tall is tall?

1 Arrange the students standing alongside each other, from the shortest child to the tallest. Ask the class if the person at the tallest end is tall. If they say 'yes', ask them if a basketball player (e.g. Michael Jordan) were to stand next to this person, would she/he still be considered tall?

2 How do we measure if something is tall or short?

    In this discussion, key points to consider are *tall* and *height*.

SESSION FIVE: WHAT IS RUDE?

Alice looked all round the table, but there was nothing on it but tea. 'I don't see any wine,' she remarked.

'There isn't any,' said the March Hare.

'Then it wasn't very civil of you to offer it,' said Alice angrily.

'It wasn't very civil of you to sit down without being invited,' said the March Hare.

'I didn't know it was your table,' said Alice: 'it's laid for a great deal many more than three.'

'Your hair wants cutting,' said the Hatter. He had been looking at Alice for some time with great curiosity, and this was his first speech.

'You should learn not to make personal remarks,' Alice said with some severity: It's very rude.'

- Students work together to classify the following situations.

	Very rude	Somewhat rude	Not rude at all
1. Picking your nose in public	.....	.....	.....
2. Picking your nose in private	.....	.....	.....
3. Eating the last piece of cake at a party	.....	.....	.....
4. Calling out in class	.....	.....	.....
5. Asking your teacher to raise his/ her hand when they wish to speak	.....	.....	.....
6. Crying in front of your friend	.....	.....	.....
7. Crying alone in your bedroom	.....	.....	.....
8. Telling your Mum you don't want any dinner	.....	.....	.....
9. Asking someone to marry you	.....	.....	.....
10. Doing your shopping with only your bathers on	.....	.....	.....
11. Talking to your dog in public	.....	.....	.....

SESSION SIX: WORDS AND MEANINGS

'Do you mean that you think you can find out the answer to it?' said the March Hare.

'Exactly so,' said Alice.

'Then you should say what you mean,' the March Hare went on.

'I do,' Alice hastily replied; 'at least — I mean what I say — that's the same thing, you know.'

'Not the same thing a bit!' said the Hatter. 'Why, you might just as well say that "I see what I eat" is the same thing as "I eat what I see"!'

'You might just as well say,' added the March Hare, 'that "I like what I get" is the same thing as "I get what I like"!'

'You might just as well say,' added the Dormouse ... 'that "I breathe when I sleep", is the same thing as "I sleep when I breathe"!'

1 Discuss whether these statements are the same. If so, why? If not, why not?

2 Each student then writes down their own examples of two statements that can change in meaning by rearranging some of the words within the statement. Volunteers give examples of their ideas.

SESSION SEVEN: QUESTIONS AND ANSWERS

The Hatter opened his eyes very wide ... but all he said was, 'why is a raven like a writing desk?' ...

'Have you guessed the riddle yet?' said the Hatter.

'No, I give up,' Alice replied. 'What's the answer?'

'I haven't the slightest idea,' said the Hatter.

'Nor I,' said the March Hare.

Alice sighed wearily. 'I think you might do something better with the time,' she said, 'than wasting it in asking riddles that have no answers.'

1 Read the extract aloud and then ask:
   Do riddles need to have answers?
   Do all questions have answers?

Does a question need to have a corresponding answer for it to be called a question?

2 Students work together to list the following into one of the three categories provided.

	Definite answer	Unknown answer	No real answer
1. The number of people on earth	.....	.....	.....
2. The number of stars in the sky	.....	.....	.....
3. The age of the universe	.....	.....	.....
4. To be happy	.....	.....	.....
5. The size of a thought	.....	.....	.....
6. The existence of ghosts	.....	.....	.....
7. The age of white	.....	....	.....
8. The color of jealousy	.....	.....	.....
9. The length of a line	....	.....	.....
10. The number of corners in a circle	.....	.....	.....
11. The 'smartest' person on earth	.....	.....	.....

SESSION EIGHT: WHAT IS TIME?

'If you knew Time as well as I do,' said the Hatter, 'you wouldn't talk about wasting *it*. It's *him*.'

- Questions for discussion:
  What is time?
  Can we stop time?
  Was there such a thing as time before humans invented clocks/sundials?
  Was there such a thing as time before humans?
  Was time invented or was it always there?
  Students could be placed in five groups, given one of the questions to examine, and then asked to tell the class what they decided.

Fantastic Mr Fox
by Roahl Dahl

A unit of work for years 3 - 4
by Alexandra Walker

Following is a summary of *Fantastic Mr Fox*.

> *Fantastic Mr Fox* is the story of the battle between the Fox family and three wealthy but very mean farmers. Farmer Boggis was a chicken farmer, Farmer Bunce was a duck and goose farmer and Farmer Bean was a turkey and apple farmer. In their own ways, they were all greedy, bad tempered and selfish.
>
> Mr Fox kept his family well fed by stealing chickens, ducks, geese and turkeys from the three farmers. The stealing enraged the farmers who were always being tricked by clever Mr Fox. However, Farmer Bean found Mr Fox's den, and the three farmers set out to catch him. They staked out the den and succeeded in shooting off Mr Fox's tail but they did not catch him. They then decided to starve out the foxes by keeping a watch on the entrance to the den. They waited and waited, but there was no sign of a fox. In their frustration they argued and quarrelled and eventually they decided to dig out the foxes. They used huge digging machines, but could not find the foxes.
>
> The starving foxes had also begun to dig. Mr Fox realised that he could enter Boggis's chicken shed by digging down the hill and up underneath the shed. He caught enough chickens for a feast, and carefully replaced the boards so that Boggis would never notice. While tunnelling, Mr Fox meets the Badger and Weasel families who had also become trapped underground by the three farmers. Fox knew he was the one who had caused the problems, so he invited the other animals to share their feast. With Badger's help, they began tunnelling again and reached Bunce's storehouse where they stole more food. They then dug into Bean's Secret Cider Cellar and the ingredients for the feast were complete. The animals all had a huge feast underground while the farmers continued to wait and wonder.

UNIT AIMS AND OVERVIEW

The ultimate aim of philosophical inquiry in the classroom is to promote the higher level of thinking of students. The aims of this unit are:

- to encourage students to explore issues that challenge the intellect and the imagination
- to develop students' reasoning skills
- to refine students' discussion skills through ensuring the class becomes a community of inquiry

The unit contains questions that can challenge the students through a development of their thinking skills (i.e. reasoning, inquiry, concept formation, translation and critical dispositions). They also have the opportunity to question their own values, morals and rights, and those of the community in which they live.

The unit is based on issues which are mostly non-threatening to the students. It is important in this area to be sensitive to the needs of the children. Despite their ever-inquiring minds, some children may find it difficult to discuss life after death and other very personal issues.

There are a number of potential topics that can be taken from *Fantastic Mr Fox*:

- What does a mean person look like?
- Can stealing be acceptable in specific circumstances?
- When animals take food from humans should that be described as stealing?
- Should foxes be shot?
- Should introduced species in Australia like the rabbit, cane toad and fox be shot or killed in other ways to reduce their numbers?
- What does it mean to be frightened? Can you feel safe and feel frightened at the same time?
- Are monsters imaginary or real?
- Should animals be able to live where they want?
- Darkness. Night. Dreaming.
- Here to there. Can there be here?
- If foxes, badgers, moles, rabbits and weasels speak different languages, how could they understand one another?
- Could humans live underground for ever?
- Is there a story behind a story?

The best seating arrangement would be students sitting in a circle or a semi-circle, so that all children and the teacher can see and hear each other.

The teacher's role is to guide the discussion back onto its original path if necessary, to build philosophical thinking and to ensure all students have the opportunity to speak within the community of inquiry.

SESSION ONE

> *Boggis and Bunce and Bean*
> *One fat, one short one lean*
> *These horrible crooks*
> *So different in looks*
> *Were nonetheless equally mean.*

Ask the children to read the above poem through together. Ask the students if there are any questions they would like to ask about this poem.

Discussion

1 Are all crooks horrible?

   If students would like to discuss this issue, ensure the question is written where all students can read it and reflect upon it.

   Perhaps initially ask the student who posed the question what they think, then let the other students bounce ideas off one another.

2 What does a mean person look like?

   Many students have a preconceived idea that all mean people are ugly.

   Place a very large piece of butchers paper and textas on the floor in the centre of the children.

   Give students the opportunity to discuss their perceived ideas on what mean people look like. If the children want to they can use the butchers paper to write words or draw pictures to assist them in their discussion. If there are a large number of students in the class, divide them into several groups which can then come together to share their discussions. It is important that the students have sufficient time to debate newly formed and/or challenged ideas about what a mean person may look like.

3 If someone behaves in a mean way, does that show they are mean?

SESSION TWO

> Suddenly Badger said, 'Doesn't this worry you just a tiny bit, Foxy?'
>   'Worry me?' said Mr Fox. 'What?'
>   'All this ... this stealing.'
>   Mr Fox stopped digging and stared at Badger as though he had gone completely dotty. 'My dear old furry frump,' he said, 'do you know anyone in the whole world who wouldn't swipe a few chickens if his children were starving to death?'

- Ask the children to read pages 70 and 71 from *Fantastic Mr Fox* together.
- Give students the opportunity to ask questions which arise from readings.
- When students initially start asking questions, some may be factual and some philosophical. If factual questions are asked, explain to students that these questions are important and direct students to places where they can find the answers i.e. the text itself, or the reference section in the school library, etc.

Possible questions

1 Can stealing be acceptable (in specific circumstances)?
2 When animals take food from humans, should that be described as stealing?

Possible ways of developing philosophical inquiry

1 If the students had a majority vote on question one, the issue could be debated using De Bono's six hats method. The students could all be numbered off one to six, with the numbers meaning the students are required to debate in the following way:
   1. black = negative
   2. white = all factual
   3. red = emotional
   4. blue = overall view
   5. green = new perspective
   6. yellow = positive

Once the students have their number and color, organise them into color groups around the room, giving each student a matching hat. Each group will need butchers paper and textas to write down ideas and possibly initial guidance from their teacher if students are unfamiliar with this technique.

Once the students have had sufficient time in their discussion groups, they can select a spokesperson to represent their group or they can all sit together within the semicircle forum and share their groups ideas on whether stealing can be acceptable (in specific circumstances).

SESSION THREE

Bean picked his nose delicately with a long finger. 'I have a plan,' he said.
'You've never had a decent plan yet,' said Bunce.
'Shut up and listen,' said Bean. 'Tomorrow night we will all hide just outside the hole where the fox lives. We will wait there until he comes

out. Then ... Bang! Bang-bang-bang.'
'Very clever,' said Bunce. 'But first we shall have to find the hole.'
'My dear Bunce, I've already found it,' said the crafty Bean. 'It's up in the wood on the hill. It's under a huge tree ...'

Questions
- Is Bean's behavior appropriate?
- Should the foxes be shot?
- Do the foxes have rights?

Have a hat with folded pieces of paper inside. Walk around the room and ask children to take a piece of paper. Each piece should have a specific character to play, i.e. Mr or Mrs Fox, the baby foxes, farmers (possibly Boggis, Bunce and Bean), environmentalists, animal protectionists and individuals who make goods from fox fur as a living.

Ask the children to write a few sentences on how their character would react to foxes being shot.

Create several small plays so all the children can express how they think their character might react. How do the plays end?

SESSION FOUR

'... What was that?' He turned his head sharply and listened. The noise he heard now was the most frightening noise a fox can ever hear — the scrape-scrape-scraping of shovels digging into the soil. 'Wake up!' he shouted. 'They're digging us out!' Mrs Fox was wide awake in one second. She sat up quivering all over. 'Are you sure that's it?' she whispered.

'I'm positive! Listen.'

They'll kill my children!' cried Mrs Fox.

'Never!' said Mr Fox.

'But darling, they will!' sobbed Mrs Fox. 'You know they will!'

Scrunch, scrunch, scrunch went the shovels above their heads. Small stones and bits of earth began falling from the roof of the tunnel.

'How will they kill us, Mummy?' asked one of the small foxes. His round black eyes were huge with fright. 'Will there be dogs?' he said.

Mrs Fox began to cry. She gathered her four children close to her and held them tight.

Questions
- What does it mean to be frightened?
- Can you feel safe and feel frightened at the same time?

- Can being frightened prevent you from doing things?
- Can you think of something you didn't do because you were afraid?
- Can you think of something you didn't do out of fear and you were glad you didn't?
- What things is it okay to be afraid of? What is it silly to be afraid of?

These questions help children to extend their thoughts on being frightened, particularly the first question. After the students have examined their own lives, encourage them to look at fright from an animal perspective. Would animals experience similar emotions to humans? Encourage students to listen carefully to one another, and to respond to one another.

SESSION FIVE

> Soon two enormous caterpillar tractors with mechanical shovels on their front ends came clanking into the wood. Bean was driving one. Bounce the other. The machines were both black. They were murderous, brutal-looking monsters.

Questions and discussion

1 Are monsters imaginary or real?

Children are always fascinated by monsters thus, despite other topics arising from their reading of *Fantastic Mr Fox*, the students at some stage will probably wish to pursue this question on monsters. Give each student a piece of paper with a line down the centre of the page. Ask the students to think carefully about the words *imaginary monster* and *real monster*. Ask them to then make a drawing of an imaginary monster and a real monster.

2 After the students have had time to complete their drawings encourage/initiate a discussion in the following areas.

Were all the students able to draw an imaginary and a real monster? If they couldn't, why not?

Did any of the students' pictures contradict one another? (For example, the Loch Ness Monster is believed to be both real and imaginary by different people.)

Can you touch or look at any of the monsters?

Can you only think about others?

Pin all the pictures on a wall and give the students an opportunity to look at them. Encourage debate and questioning from all students. Note whether opinions change and how these changes in opinion evolved. Are changes substantiated through others' comments?

SESSION SIX

Now there began a desperate race, the machines against the foxes. In the beginning, the hill looked like this ... After about an hour, as the machines bit away more and more soil from the hilltop, it looked like this ...

Questions and activities

1 Should animals be able to live where they want without being threatened?

Ask all the students to think of an animal. Once they have, give them a sticky label so they can write the animal's name down and stick it on their front.

Inform the children they're going to play a game of survival. Around the room have signs that have specific types of food and shelter written on them i.e. rabbit hole may be close to grass, etc. These signs will have to be covered until students have selected their animals. If the students can't find food or shelter for the animal they are by walking around the room, then other animals can prey on them if it would happen in the wild i.e. a cat may catch a bird, a fox may catch a chicken. The outcome of this will be natural attrition — some animals will be safe yet others will be preyed upon.

After a few students have been removed, reintroduce them as humans with nothing being safe. What ultimately occurs?

2 Discuss with students how they felt initially (depending upon their chosen animal) and how they felt when humans were introduced. Possible focus may reflect upon human destruction of many animals' habitats.

Are our homes where theirs used to be?

Should we be more understanding of different animal's needs? Encourage students to listen to one another, reflect upon comments then respond in appropriate ways.

CHAPTER SIX

Changed Approaches: Establishing Philosophy in Schools

Preparation of teachers

Philosophical inquiry through a community of inquiry model was not part of most teachers' initial training. Professional development workshops, which vary in length and approach, are available, and usually include the following:

- **Discussion of the nature of the community of inquiry**. Questions like 'How is a philosophical discussion different from other discussions?' and 'What is distinctive about the approach of philosophy in the classroom to moral and ethical issues?' need to be discussed and demonstrated. Teachers need to understand how philosophical inquiry differs from their everyday questioning.

- **Examination of a range of texts** specially written for philosophical inquiry. (e.g. de Haan, McColl & McCutcheon 1995; Cam 1994; Sprod 1993; Lipman, various). These provide an excellent source of both theory and philosophy. Modelling how to use these resources is a vital component of teacher workshops.

- **The involvement of participants in philosophical discussions.** Immersion should be the paramount experience. Teacher confidence in handling a rigorous discussion can be built through practice. Raising philosophical issues from stories is one aspect. Recognising and encouraging good questions, those which foster philosophical inquiry, is another. Workshop participants can practise these skills by leading one or two workshop sessions.

- If workshops are held once a week for a month, **teachers can practise the skills learned in their classrooms** and discuss experiences at a later session. Their recognition of the many ways philosophical inquiry enriches classroom work through experience also enriches workshop discussions.

- Once strategies and approaches are understood, and if a group of students can be organised, a session with students presents a great opportunity for teachers to practise skills learned. They can **prepare a session, and then, together with the trainer, run a class.** 'Trainees' can contribute with questions or comments when they feel comfortable.

- The teacher trainer normally provides **strategies for teachers** to avoid a common tendency in early sessions to:
  - dominate the discussion
  - not involve sufficient students in a discussion
  - allow a few participants to dominate the discussion
  - not keep a discussion focused long enough for philosophical insight to begin to emerge
  - not ask clarifying questions, or make sure the issue at hand is understood by all members of the group
  - hold back from discussion so that they are not facilitating the discussion sufficiently

- **Modelling ways of clarifying questions, involving all students in a discussion, and quietening dominators** as the session progresses is vital. Discussion of teachers' concerns about questions like 'What was happening here?', or 'Why do you think the discussion faltered?' is also important. A trusting environment needs to have been established between trainer and teacher.

The role of modelling

Theoretical issues will arise as the teachers do their classroom work in the early months. Ideally, when teachers start taking philosophy with their classes, the responsibility should be shared by the teacher and the trainer. Together they can lead or follow up the questioning, delving further into particular areas of personal interest. This means that the trainer and teacher will be involved in discussions which include questions like, 'Where could I have ...?' or 'Did you notice that ...?' or 'Wasn't it interesting when ...?' or 'I really didn't do that very well'. The students enjoy watching the teachers working together, and discussing teaching points in front of them.

In the early stages teachers often work in pairs with groups of students. For example, two teachers may team teach one class when the opportunity presents itself. With the support of colleagues and trainers they see how quickly a community of inquiry builds. Sound preparation and evaluation of early sessions is important. This includes familiarity with the philosophical issues and thinking skills encouraged by the resources being used.

Once teachers understand and foster philosophical inquiry they commonly describe the following changes in their classrooms

- more satisfying and rigourous discussions
- wider participation of class members
- questioning being valued
- 'the' answer no longer being sought
- the transfer of skills to other curriculum areas

Teacher preparation

The following professional development sessions held in one school reflect some of the ways post-initial teacher education in philosophical inquiry is occurring.

1 STAFF INTRODUCTORY SESSION

This half-day session introduced staff to the main aims of, and reasons for, introducing philosophical inquiry. Teachers already involved in using philosophical inquiry described teaching strategies and changes to student involvement in their classrooms.

A critical point made was the rigor with which the logic/reasoning skills are approached and the choice of resources which enable this. Prior to dividing them into groups, the notion of a community of inquiry was demonstrated via a range of 'thinking' exercises.

Giving teachers an accurate idea of what is involved requires a longer session or, better still, a few sessions, or demonstration lessons.

2 PRIMARY STAFF WORKSHOP

Four two-hour sessions, once a week after school, is an approach preferred by both teachers and trainers, and was the format chosen by the school.

The anecdotes of a staff member who had worked with philosophy in her classroom for one and a half years were of considerable assistance during the sessions. As philosophical inquiry classroom approaches were discussed, she was able to inject details about her own classes where the issues being discussed had been raised.

A variety of philosophical texts and resources were examined, ranging from specifically written materials to news items and videos. The teachers trialled procedures during the intervening weeks and discussed their experiences at the next session. This sharing included details of student participation and the kinds of discourse in which they had been involved, for example: the way conversations developed, conceptual blocks noticed, and the different kinds of thinking demonstrated during sessions.

Parent information sessions

At a parent information night the teachers and trainer spoke of the school's educational reasons for introducing philosophical inquiry. Parents were already interested and supportive, describing the challenging philosophical discussions which were occurring at home as a result of the program.

Teachers involved parents in activities and approaches which demonstrated communities of inquiry. Videotapes of sessions involving their children in philosophy sessions were shown. This participatory mode demystified the term 'philosophy' for parents and demonstrated the rigor of discussions.

Sustaining the change: Coordination and networks

An important aspect of a school's commitment to introducing philosophical inquiry into the curriculum is the presence of a coordinator who, via the school's professional development program, can guide its introduction and usage. Their role should be primarily to support teachers involved in the introduction of philosophical inquiry and to maintain contact with teacher educators if teachers have attended workshops.

Most teachers attend professional development workshops prior to establishing a community of inquiry. The teacher educators, or the school coordinator, should then try to visit them, either to observe them taking an early session with their class, or to team teach. After each session, progress and strategies for future classes can be discussed.

Keeping a journal is a good way of tracking progress. They provide a guide for future practice, a focus for discussions with colleagues, and a record of procedure when using the same resource materials with a new group of students.

It is a good idea for teachers to visit other schools to observe established communities of inquiry. Local networks which offer an exchange of ideas with other teachers have been established in many districts. Teachers appreciate the opportunity to talk about issues that emerge and perplex on an informal basis. Sharing ideas and concerns is worthwhile. Decisions about future ways of proceeding, based on other teachers' descriptions of sessions, can then be made.

The natural networking of schools in a geographical area, particularly primary schools, means that ideas spread from school to school via teachers, children and parents. The interest and involvement of teachers has a 'ripple effect'. The enthusiasm of the students and teachers involved in philosophical inquiry prompts other staff to watch sessions in progress and they often become involved in the discussions. Students enjoy the involvement by two or more staff in their discussions. A curriculum change which spreads from teacher to teacher, and later becomes part of a school policy is a better model for effective curriculum change than 'top-down' initiative.

Because there are constant changes being proposed for teachers and schools, any curriculum innovation being proposed must be plausible and have recognisable benefits. The introduction of philosophical inquiry into existing curriculum and timetables has been a successful because it is easily integrated into existing programs.

Useful Classroom Resources

Throughout the book, specifically written texts designed to foster classroom inquiry have been referred to. The following texts represent diverse approaches and are suitable for a variety of levels.

Cam, P. *Thinking Stories 1 & 2,* Hale & Ironmonger, Sydney,1993. (Each series consists of a teacher resource and activity book.)

DeHaan, C. MacColl, S. & Mc Cutcheon, L. *Philosophy with Kids 1–3,* Longman, Melbourne, 1995.

Sprod, T. *Books Into Ideas: A Community of Inquiry,* Hawker Brownlow, Melbourne, 1993.

Professor Matthew Lipman's texts, below, were created around his *Philosophy For Children* program, published in New Jersey by the International Association for Philosophy For Children. (Available from the Australian Centre for Educational Research, Hawthorn). They are listed here in approximate order of difficulty.

Elfie: Getting our Thoughts Together. (1988)
Kio and Gus: Wondering at the World. (1986)
Pixie: Looking for Meaning. (1980)
Harry Stottlemeier's Discovery: Philosophical Inquiry. (1974)
Lisa: Ethical Inquiry. (1976)
Suki: Writing: How and Why. (1978)
Mark: Social Inquiry. (1980)

Contacts for Further Information

The teacher training models described in Chapter 6 represent some approaches found to be successful by trainers in Australia. Numerous bodies representing a variety of approaches, from formal qualifications to informal professional development programs, exist in countries around the world. They offer assistance to teachers in the area of philosophical inquiry.

The following list is by no means exhaustive, but is a starting point for teachers wanting to follow up the content of this book.

AUSTRALIA

TeeCH Project, Faculty of Education, University of Melbourne, Parkville, Victoria 3052. Phone: 03 9344 8695 Fax: 03 9437 3916 (Susan Wilks)

School of Philosophy, University of NSW, PO Box 1, Kensington NSW 2033. Phone: 02 9385 2372 Fax: 02 9385 1029 (Phil Cam)

Philosophy Department, University of Queensland, St Lucia Qld 4072. Phone 07 3365 2804 Fax 07 3365 1968 (Gil Burgh)

South Australian Philosophy for Children Association, PO Box 91, Magill SA 5072. Phone 08 9302 4533 Fax 08 9332 6122 (Peter Woolcock)

Department of Education, University of Tasmania, PO Box 1214 Launceston Tas 7250. Phone: 03 6323 4287 Fax: 03 6323 4048 (Peter Davson-Galle)

Faculty of Communications, University of Canberra, PO Box 1, Belconnen ACT 2616. Phone: 02 6201 2341 Fax: 02 6201 5119 (Christine Shade)

Victorian Philosophy for Children Association, Philosophy Department, La Trobe University, Bundoora Vic 3083. Phone 03 9479 2141 Fax 03 9479 1700 (Ross Phillips)

The West Australian Philosophy for Children Association, Department of Education, Edith Cowan University, Perth WA. Phone: 08 9380 2431 Fax: 08 9380 1056 (Felicity Haynes)

USA

President, NAACI, Viterbo College, 815 9th Street, La Crosse, WI 54601. Phone: 608 784 5707 Fax: 608 791 0367 (Richard Morehouse)

Creative and Critical Teaching Center, Texas Wesleyan University, 1201 Wesleyan Avenue, Forth Worth, Texas TX 76105 (Ron Reed)

Department of Philosophy , University of Hawaii, 2530 Dole Street, Honolulu HI 96822 (Thomas Jackson)

Department of Human Environmental Sciences, University of Western Carolina, Cullowhee, North Carolina NC 28723 (David Kennedy)

University of North Carolina-Greensboro, 318 Curry, Greensboro, NC 27412 (Tony Johnson)

Philosophy for Children, Northwest, Western Oregon State College, Monmouth OR 97361 (Dale Cannon)

CANADA

Vancouver Institute of Philosophy for Children, 607W 53rd Avenue, Vancouver BC V6P 1K2. Phone: 604 322 1141 Fax 604 322 1151 (Susan Gardner)

Faculty of Philosophy, Laval University, Quebec City, Quebec G1K 7P4 (Michel Sasseville)

Faculty of Education, University of Lethbridge, 4401 University Drive, Lethbridge, Alberta T1K 3M4 (David Smith)

Faculty of Education, University of Western Ontario, 1137 Western Road, London , Ontario N6G 1G7 (Ivor Goodson)

UK

Centre for Thinking Skills, Brunel University, Twickenham, Middlesex TW1 IPT. Phone 081 891 0121 Fax: 081 568 8741 (Robert Fisher)

NEW ZEALAND

Philosophy Department, Massey University, Private Bag 11-222, Palmerston North 5330. Phone: 646 350 5136 Fax: 646 350 5676 James Battye)

Philosophy Department, University of Auckland, Private Bag 92-019, Auckland. Fax 649 373 7408 (Vanya Kovach)

SINGAPORE

Nanyang Technological University National Institute of Education, 469 Bukit Timah Road, Singapore 1025. Phone: 65 460 5254 Fax: 65 468 7945 (Lim Tock Keng)

References and Further Reading

Angus, Lawrence B. 1992 'Quality schooling, conservative education policy and educational change in Australia'. *Journal of Education Policy*, vol. 7. no. 4.

Bloom, B. S. et al. 1956. *Taxonomy of Educational Objectives 1: Cognitive Domain.* McKay, New York.

Cherednichenko, B. F. & Wilks, S. E. 1992. 'Observed changes in teaching thinking skills following training in the community of inquiry approach'. Faculty of Education, University of Melbourne.

Cherednichenko, B. F. & Wilks, S. E. 1993. 'Identifying implications of approaches to the teaching of thinking'. Faculty of Education, University of Melbourne.

Dewey, J. 1897. 'My Pedagogic Creed', in *The Philosophy of John Dewey,* ed. John J. McDermott. University of Chigaco Press, Chicago.

Dewey, J. 1897. *Democracy and Education.* Free Press.

De Bono, E. 1975. *CoRT.* W. D. Scott & Co, London. (1995, Elsevier, New York)

De Bono, E. 1976. *Teaching Thinking,* Penguin, Melbourne.(1976, Viking Penguin, New York)

Duska, R. & Whelan, M. 1975. *Moral Development: A Guide to Piaget and Kohlberg.* Paulist Press, New York.

Echeverria, E. 1990. Teaching, learning and using critical thinking. Paper presented at Philosophy for Children: East and West Conference, Taiwan.

Fisher, R. 1990. *Teaching Children to Think.* Basil Blackwell, Oxford.

Glaser, J. 1989. 'Evaluating philosophy: The Emanual School', *Philosophy for Schools Newsletter.* Australian Council for Educational Research, Melbourne.

Jackson, T. 1989. 'Teacher training: The preferred format' *Analytic Teaching,* vol. 10., no. 2. Texas Wesleyan University, Fort Worth.

Jackson, T. 1990. 'Philosophy for children training manual'. Department of Philosophy, University of Hawaii.

Lipman, M. 1985. 'Philosophy for children and critical thinking'. *National Forum,* vol. 65, no. 1.

Lipman, M. 1985. 'Thinking skills fostered by philosophy for children' in J. W. Segal, S. F. Chipman & R. Glaser (eds), *Thinking and Learning Skills, Vol. 1 : Relating Instruction to Research,* IEA, New Jersey.

Lipman, M. 1988. *Philosophy Goes to School.* Temple University Press, Philadelphia.

Lipman, M. 1990. Strengthening reasoning and judgement through philosophy for children. Paper presented at the Philosophy for Children: East and West Conference, Taiwan.

Lipman, M., Sharp, A. M. & Oscanyan F. 1980. *Philosophy in the Classroom,* 2nd ed. Temple University Press, Philadelphia.

Northfield, J. 1988, 'The change process: Achieving the vision'. The Independent Association of Registered Teachers of Victoria lecture series; Improving the Quality of Learning.

O'Laughlin, M. 1991. 'Teaching thinking skills through discussion: Towards a method of evaluation'. *Educational Philosophy and Theory,* vol. 32, no. 1.

Paul, R. 1993. *Critical Thinking.* Hawker Brownlow, Melbourne.

Peirce, C. S. 1960–1965. *The Collected Papers.* Belknap Press of Harvard University.

Perrott, C. 1988. *Classroom Talk and Pupil Learning.* Harcourt Brace Jovanovich, Sydney.

Perrott, C. 1990. Analysis of the discourse in some regular primary classrooms, and in some philosophy sessions. Paper presented at Philosophy of Education Society of Australasia Conference, Melbourne.

Piaget, J. 1964. *The Child's Conception of the World.* Routledge and Kegan, New York.

Piaget, J. 1928. *Judgement and Reasoning in the Child.* Harcourt Brace, New York.

Reed, R. F. 1987. 'Philosophy for children: Some problems', *Analytic Teaching*, vol. 8. no. 1. Texas Wesleyan University, Fort Worth.

Reed, R. F. 1992. *When We Talk We Learn*. Analytic Teaching Press, Wisconsin.

Sharp, A. M. & Reed R. F, 1992. *Studies in Philosophy for Children: Harry Stottlemeir's Discovery*, Temple University Press, Philadelphia.

Splitter, L. 1987. 'Philosophy for children: The community of inquiry and thinking about thinking'. Australian Council for Educational Research Melbourne.

Splitter, L. 1988. 'On teaching children to be better thinkers'. *Unicorn: The Journal of the Australian College of Education*.

Victorian Ministry of Education 1984. *Curriculum Development & Planning.* Ministerial Paper No. 6. Ministry of Education, Melbourne.

Victorian Ministry of Education 1988. *School Curriculum and Organisation Framework*. Ministry of Education, Melbourne.

Victorian Ministry of Education 1989. *Learning How To Learn*. Ministry of Education, Melbourne.

Whalley, M. 1989. 'Philosophy for Children' in M. J. Coles, & W. D. Robinson, *Teaching Thinking*, Bristol Press.

Wilks, S. E. 1992. An evaluation of Lipman's Philosophy for Children Program. M.Ed thesis, Faculty of Education, University of Melbourne.

Wilks, S. E. 1993. 'Values in the classroom.' *Education Quarterly Australia* (Spring 1993) Curriculum Corporation, Melbourne.

Wilks, S. E. 1993 'A community of enquiry'. *Primary Education*, vol. 5, Collins Dove, Melbourne.

Wilks, S. E. 1993 'Reinforcing teacher training for philosophy in schools'. *Bulletin of the International Council for Philosophical Inquiry with Children*. vol 8, no. 2. Centro De Filosofia Para Ninos, Spain.

Wilks, S. E. 1993. 'Reflection on the implementation of philosophy into school curricula as a change process', *Analytic Teaching*, vol. 14, no 1. Published by Viterbo College, Wisconsin, USA.

Wilks, S. E. 1993. 'Teacher self-reported changes in classroom practice and student outcome: Training in improving student questioning and thinking'. University of Melbourne.

Wilks, S. E. 1994. 'Encouraging pupil participation: Establishing a community of inquiry.' *Critical and Creative Thinking.* vol. 1, no. 4. Deakin University Press, Geelong.

Index

More books from Heinemann

Thinking for Themselves
Developing Strategies for Reflective Learning
Jeni Wilson and Lesley Wing Jan

By encouraging children to think about their learning and to become aware of and control their thinking processes, teachers can help them become active, responsible learners who can make their own decisions, choose appropriate strategies, assess their own work and set their own goals.

Contents: Getting started; Developing the appropriate learning environment; Program planning; Negotiating with students; Questioning and self-assessment techniques.
ISBN 0 435 08805 X   156 pp

The Collaborative Classroom
A Guide to Co-operative Learning
Susan and Tim Hill

The Collaborative Classroom is a creative and practical guide for teachers who want to implement and gain maximum benefit for students from co-operative learning. The book focuses on and identifies the areas where co-operative skills are needed: forming groups and managing differences. *The Collaborative Classroom* is both practical and encouraging and includes dozens of activities to get the beginning teacher started.
ISBN 0 435 08525 5   162 pp

Responsive Evaluation
Making Valid Judgments about Student Literacy
Edited by Brian Cambourne and Jan Turbill

Changes in teaching practice caused by new understandings of how children learn have made many traditional methods of evaluation obsolete. Demands to demonstrate accountability put pressure on teachers to devise new methods of assessment which demonstrate accountability and are appropriate to current teaching methods.

Responsive Evaluation presents approaches which lead to optimum learning, reflect holistic thinking, enrich classroom teaching and are seen to be rigorous, scientific and valid.

Jan Turbill and Brian Cambourne have worked with teachers, principals, academics, parents and students to establish assessment procedures. All have contributed to *Responsive Evaluation* and report on how they put the theory in to practice.
ISBN 0 435 08829 7   176 pp

I Teach
A Guide to Inspiring Classroom Leadership
Joan Dalton and Julie Boyd

Specific and practical insights into the 'what' and 'how' of effective learning and teaching presented succinctly and visually.

Contents: Identify your goals; Walk the leader's walk; Build relationships with others; Create a community of learners; Empower growth in others; Work on self- growth: identify personal strengths, highlight areas for self-improvement and plan for balanced leadership.
ISBN 0 435 08782 7   128 pp

Becoming Responsible Learners
Strategies for Positive Classroom Management
Joan Dalton and Mark Collis

Becoming Responsible Learners is an invaluable asset to teachers who want to encourage children to take responsibility for their own learning and behaviour. An extremely practical and highly readable book presenting strategies and guide-lines for classroom management, this best-selling book is the result of observing effective collaborative teachers at work and talking to them about their beliefs and classroom practices.
ISBN 0 435 08568 9   80 pp

The Big Picture
Integrating students' learning
Edited by Marilyn Woolley and Keith Pigdon

The Big Picture addresses the key issues which are central to the idea of the integrated curriculum and translates them into practical classroom advice.

Contents: Context and framework: the ideas which drive teachers' curriculum planning; A planning model: bringing the components together in an organised yet flexible structure; The model in practice: activities and strategies; Language and the integrated curriculum: integrated learning and specific curriculum practice; Assessment and evaluation: for the learner, the teacher and the community; Whole school change: it starts in your classroom.
ISBN 0 435 08792 4   128 pp

Write Me a Poem
Reading, Writing and Performing Poetry
Lorraine Wilson

Write Me a Poem is a very practical book for teachers interested in encouraging children to explore reading, writing and performing poetry. It includes a range of 'child-friendly' poems by published poets as a starting point for children to read, discuss, share and present poetry.

Contents: Learning to write poetry; Infants write free verse; Free verse and upper primary children; Noisy poems; Poems for two voices; Rhyme.
ISBN 0 435 08823 8   64 pp

The Home-School Connection
Guidelines for Working with Parents
Jacqueline McGilp and Maureen Michaels

The benefits of stronger ties between school and home are backed by research and acknowledged by both parents and teachers. *The Home-School Connection* takes on the challenge of getting the home and school to work together, to listen to each other and to use resources well so that effective learning for students is a reality. The book raises issues and establishes guidelines for involving the home and the wider community in educating children.

The Home-School Connection caters for a wide range of involvement, from small steps for the individual teacher to whole school strategies, and provides practical ideas and activities.
ISBN 0 435 08820 3   96pp

For information on these and other titles contact
Heinemann
361 Hanover Street, Portsmouth, NH 03801-3912
Tel   603- 431 7894   Fax 603- 431 7840